"Oh, the joy and freedom of
that are foreign to far too m
to read *Unburdened* by Vanc
pure, simple, and absolutely revolutionary reality that Jesus died for
you so that He might live in you!"

MW01004681

David Platt, pastor, McLean Bible Church

"Vance Pitman is a brilliant leader and communicator. In *Unburdened*,
he shares profound insight from the Bible, along with lessons learned
the hard way in life. He shows how a deeper experience of God's grace
can transform your relationship with God. You can walk in greater
spiritual freedom, and Vance shows the way."

Jud Wilhite, senior pastor, Central Church; author, *Pursued*

"In *Unburdened*, Vance Pitman not only reminds us that 'works' don't
work but also shows us what actually does. This is more than a book!
This is a manifesto that will help you live life to the fullest."

David Nasser, pastor, author, and speaker

"This book is gold. Solid gold. It is like breathing a breath of fresh
air for the first time after living in a world of pollution all our lives.
*Unburdened* reminds us to stop working so hard, bound by the exhausting and burdensome rules of religion, and instead allow the life
of Jesus to take over our own. Thank you, Vance Pitman. Thank you
for this refreshment to my soul. Thank you for this book."

Thom S. Rainer, founder and CEO, Church
Answers; author, *I Am a Church Member*

"The burning question throughout Vance's book is this: What does
it look like to faithfully follow Jesus? It is of great importance that
every generation answer this question and frame what this looks like
within our cultural milieu. We live in a cultural moment that depends
on how Christians answer this question and will lead to either redun-
dancy or a revival of the Christian faith. I'm thankful for this book

and know it will help you love God more faithfully, appreciate God's family more deeply, and be intentional with ministry in the world as ambassadors for Christ and His kingdom."

**Ed Stetzer**, Wheaton College

"Vance gives a fresh, compelling vision of the life of discipleship. He's not only one of the most effective pastors I've observed but also one of the godliest people I've ever known. His spirit comes through on every page of this book! You'll be challenged, convicted, and inspired as you read it."

**J. D. Greear**, pastor, The Summit Church; president, The Southern Baptist Convention; author, *Above All*

"I'm so excited about *Unburdened* and the freedom it will bring to so many in their walk with Christ. Vance Pitman has a real gift in communicating the simplicity of following Jesus. This book is long overdue!"

**Pat Williams**, cofounder, Orlando Magic; author, *Character Carved in Stone*

"I must admit that I had mixed emotions while reading the life-changing book *Unburdened* from my friend Vance Pitman. On one hand, I was truly excited for a book that talks about the importance of relationships in every believer's life, but on the other hand, I was burdened that I did not have a book like this when I was a babe in Christ! As a young believer, my nickname could have been "Repentance" because of how I messed up and asked for God's forgiveness on a regular basis. I was trying to live *for* God instead of allowing God to live *through* me. I encourage every believer to read this book, but especially those of you who are burdened with trying to do it all on your own. I assure you, this book will set you free!"

**Fred Luter Jr.**, pastor, Franklin Avenue Baptist Church; former president, Southern Baptist Convention

"*Unburdened* will serve as a readable and refreshing source of instruction for Christ-followers in their various stages of discipleship. Encouraging renewed and strengthened relationships with the Triune God, members of the community of faith, and others, Vance Pitman offers helpful guidance and direction from his own experience and his reflections on the biblical text. Many who are entrapped by legalism will find *Unburdened* to be a revitalizing resource."

**David S. Dockery**, chancellor, Trinity International University

"Every generation needs to be reminded of the truth about abiding and living in the power of the Holy Spirit. These pages are filled with truth about relationships. Our relationship with the Lord is essential if we are to live out our faith in power. Call it what you want—the victorious Christian life, the Spirit-filled life, or the Christ life—*Unburdened* will open your heart and mind to all God has in store for believers who simply take Him at His Word. Let the truth revealed on these pages unburden you from trying to be better. Let it liberate you as you embrace the joy of being a Christ-follower."

**Michael Catt**, pastor, Sherwood Church;
founder, ReFresh Conference

"Vance is a gifted leader and preacher who has led many to find joy in Jesus and experience the free, unburdened life of following Him. I am thankful for Vance and his book."

**Eric Geiger**, senior pastor, Mariners Church

"*Unburdened* powerfully exposes Satan's crafty work in the deception of religion. Information and doing are *not* the abundant life Jesus promised. In fact, they are burdens that produce no true life or joy. This is a desperately needed book for the American religious landscape! Vance's personal transparency will set others free."

**Kathy Litton**, director of planter spouse development, North American Mission Board of the Southern Baptist Convention

"What keeps most believers from living at the full potential God intended? For some it is sin. For others, maybe fear or apathy. But I am convinced many more are sidelined by the misconception that the Christian life requires much more 'doing' from them than God ever intended. My friend Vance Pitman has discovered for himself and now shares with all of us some great news—our lives in Christ are meant to be much simpler! If more believers would put into practice what Vance teaches in *Unburdened*, their lives would be freer and more fulfilling, and they would also have a much greater impact on the lost world around them."

**Kevin Ezell**, president, North American Mission
Board of the Southern Baptist Convention

"Far too many Christians don't really believe that following Jesus means we have freedom. Too often, we trade the chains of sin for the chains of religious performance. Vance Pitman offers a clear, biblical view of what following Jesus looks like: relationship with the Father, relationships in community, and relationships toward mission. If Christianity has started to feel dull, boring, or burdensome, pick up this book and be reminded of the freedom Christ offers!"

**Matt Carter**, pastor of preaching and vision,
The Austin Stone Community Church

"Pastor Vance has the gift of relatability. *Unburdened* highlights many of my own struggles in my Christian journey. As a professional baseball player, I am being judged on performance daily. Knowing that I don't need to perform for the King, just be with Him, is an exciting paradigm shift."

**Nick Hundley**, catcher, Oakland A's

"Many well-intentioned Christ-followers find themselves exhausted from carrying an unnecessary self-inflicted burden. This inevitably leads to a weak and discouraged Christian with little fruit in their life. This is why I am delighted that Pastor Vance Pitman has written *Unburdened* to see people unshackled and set free toward the powerful, biblical life in Christ. Within our current times and culture, we desperately need the church to throw off all distractions and diversions and seek the purity and power of the Holy Spirit. This book has the potential to do just that. What I love about *Unburdened* is that it is not only true but also written by a man who lives this out personally and has witnessed thousands of lives changed through this message. Mine is one of these lives that has been wonderfully influenced through Pastor Vance. I wholeheartedly, and with urgency, commend this book. May the Lord use it powerfully in your life."

**Robbie Symons**, senior pastor, Hope Bible Church

"I don't know about you, but I run into a lot of Christians who are exhausted, burned out, and demoralized. Maybe you're one of them. For many, life seems really heavy, and the church sometimes makes it even heavier. I know no one wiser and more equipped to unburden such lives than the author of this book, Vance Pitman, one of the most effective pastors in North America. Vance calls us away from a life driven by rules and regulations and toward a life joined to and enlivened by Jesus Himself. Lay aside some burdens and listen to the joy in this book."

**Russell Moore**, president, The Ethics & Religious Liberty
Commission of the Southern Baptist Convention

"*Unburdened* simplifies what we can so easily complicate—the life of a Jesus follower. Instead of wanting to live for Jesus, I now want Jesus to live His life through me."

**Ryan Carpenter**, center, NHL Vegas Golden Knights

"We say all the time that Christianity is not about religion—it's about relationships. But we still get easily caught up in all the dos and don'ts. *Unburdened* is a clear call back to a life of abiding in Christ and experiencing freedom to the fullest."

**Dhati Lewis**, lead pastor, Blueprint Church;
vice president, Send Network

"If there is an inkling in you for something more. If you have found yourself disappointed by your immorality or morality. If there is the slightest hint that something is missing, this book is for you. My friend Vance Pitman points us to the only source of satisfaction—Jesus Christ—and winsomely reminds us that life is not about living for Jesus but about experiencing the life of Jesus lived through us!"

**Bryan Loritts**, lead pastor, Abundant Life Christian Fellowship; author, *Insider/Outsider*

"*Unburdened* is an honest, wise, moving, and loving message by my friend Vance Pitman. We will all do well to learn the lesson that following Jesus really is all about relationships! It is not about exhausting work to earn anything. Pastor Vance makes it clear that the life of a Christian is about the freedom that comes from allowing Jesus to live through us. Every person who is in relationship with Christ, or who wants to be, should read this excellent book. It will be life-changing."

**Jon Erwin**, director, *I Can Only Imagine*

"Life-changing! Soak up every life-changing truth in *Unburdened* to find the full and abundant life you're craving."

**David Chrzan**, pastor, Saddleback Church

# UNBURDENED

# UNBURDENED

## STOP LIVING FOR JESUS
## SO JESUS CAN
## LIVE THROUGH YOU

# VANCE PITMAN

BakerBooks

*a division of Baker Publishing Group*
Grand Rapids, Michigan

© 2020 by Vance Pitman

Published by Baker Books
a division of Baker Publishing Group
PO Box 6287, Grand Rapids, MI 49516-6287
www.bakerbooks.com

Printed in the United States of America

Library of Congress Cataloging-in-Publication Data
Names: Pitman, Vance, author.
Title: Unburdened : stop living for Jesus so Jesus can live through you / Vance
   Pitman.
Description: Grand Rapids : Baker Books, a division of Baker Publishing Group,
   2020.
Identifiers: LCCN 2019028441 | ISBN 9780801094613 (paperback)
Subjects: LCSH: Christian life.
Classification: LCC BV4501.3 .P578 2020 | DDC 248.4—dc23
LC record available at https://lccn.loc.gov/2019028441

Published in association with Yates & Yates, www.yates2.com.

20   21   22   23   24   25   26      7   6   5   4   3   2   1

To my wife,
Kristie,
for being the most authentic Jesus follower I know.

To my children—
Hannah, Caleb, Elijah, and Faith—
for giving me the constant joy
of watching them grow as Jesus followers.

To my faith family,
Hope Church,
for being a radical community
of Jesus followers.

# Contents

**Part 4  Share  157**

# Acknowledgments

I am deeply grateful to Jesus that, by His marvelous grace, He whispered to my soul, *"Follow Me."*

I am grateful to my wife and kids, who have joined with me on a journey for the past twenty years in Las Vegas to discover the truths contained in this book. Words cannot express how much I love you all and how each of you has helped shape the content contained in these pages.

I am grateful for my parents, who sowed the seeds into my life that ultimately led me to follow Jesus.

I am grateful to Travis Ogle for his friendship and partnership in the gospel, without which this project never would have been realized. Your encouragement, support, and insight have been invaluable in fleshing out the principles in this book for over fifteen years.

I am grateful for the pastors and staff at Hope Church, who co-labor with me daily to shepherd a fellowship to connect people to live the life of a Jesus follower.

I am grateful for Shagufta Brown, whose passion for this message and my voice, as well as her attention to detail and deadlines, have rescued me more than once on this journey.

I am grateful to Sealy Yates and his team for believing in me and in this project.

I am grateful to Brian Vos and the Baker team for embracing the message of this book from the very beginning and for working so tirelessly with me to get it to this point.

I am grateful to Sam O'Neal for his enormous assistance through the editing process.

I am grateful to Letty, Johnny, Dan, Jim, Chip, Mike, and Jeff, who helped lay the foundation to make this book possible.

I am grateful for Clyde Cranford, who for two years mentored me and first taught me to stop living for Jesus so Jesus could live through me. See you there, my friend!

# Introduction

"Where are you from?"

The man sitting next to me on the airplane had an honest face and seemed genuinely curious. But mostly he just seemed like he wanted to chat.

I smiled at his question. I spend a lot of time on airplanes, and I like it when people are willing to have a conversation rather than retreating behind their books and noise-canceling headphones for the entire flight. I especially like it when they ask me where I'm from.

"Las Vegas," I told him. Then I smiled again as the man raised his eyebrows. That answer almost always grabs people's attention.

"What do you do for a living there?"

I said the same thing I say to everyone who asks me that question: "You'll never guess in a million years."

He tried. He came up with most of the usual guesses—that I work at a casino, that I play professional poker, that I'm a chef at one of the big restaurants, and so on. One time someone asked if I was a hit man for the mob.

Eventually, I leaned a little closer to him, like I was about to share a secret. "I'm a church pastor."

"A pastor? In Las Vegas?"

"Yep." I nodded. "There's a lot of job security for my profession in Sin City."

The man was quiet for a moment, but I could tell he wanted to ask something more. "So," he said, kind of hesitantly, "what religion are you?"

I smiled again, but bigger this time. I love it when people ask me *that* question!

"Well, I'm not religious at all."

The man squinted at me a little bit, like he was trying to spot the joke. "How in the world can you be a pastor and not be religious?"

"That's easy." I met his eyes to show him there was no joke. "I don't believe in religion. I think religion drives more people away from God than anything else."

### The Burden of Religion

What comes to mind when you hear the word *religion*? What images do you see? What memories come flooding back? What emotions do you feel?

For me, the concept of "religion" brings to mind a heavy burden—a weight laid across my shoulders that constantly bogs me down and makes me collapse under the pressure. Religion is all about rules I have to follow even when they don't benefit anyone and don't make sense. Religion involves words and phrases I'm supposed to memorize and recite on command, even when I don't know what they mean or why they matter.

Religion is exhausting!

I remember my first experiences with this kind of "religion." I became a follower of Jesus when I was in college, and during that early period of my faith, I was encouraged to join an accountability group. People who cared about me told me I needed accountability from other Christians to learn what it means to live the Christian life.

Looking back, I can see the principle behind this group was good. Accountability is a helpful tool for spiritual health, and I definitely needed others to walk with me as I navigated this new way of life. Plus, as we'll explore in part three of this book, community is a wonderful blessing within the church.

So the principle of accountability is good, but the practice of that particular accountability group wasn't good. Its focus was on dos and don'ts, rights and wrongs, rules and regulations. Its focus was religion.

Every week we spent the first half of our time together "examining" one another with a list of performance-based questions. How many days this week did you read your Bible? How many hours did you pray? How many verses did you memorize? How many times did you share the gospel? Did you faithfully attend all church services and a Sunday school class? On top of these questions, I was asked about what I listened to, or what I looked at, or where I went.

As a result of this weekly examination, I quickly came to the conclusion that following Jesus was all about performance. I thought being a Christian meant constantly striving to measure up.

And I hated it. Specifically, I hated constantly carrying the burden of expectations—both my own and others'. As the group's meeting grew closer each week, I whipped myself into high gear. I wrote two or three days of journal entries all in one evening so

I could keep up appearances. I crammed memory verses into my brain the night before so I could recite them as if I'd been practicing throughout the week.

All that was bad. But the worst part was knowing that, as I walked into those gatherings, I was about to lie to ensure the rest of the group thought I was a faithful disciple. Can you imagine? The burden of measuring up as a follower of Jesus so dominated my life that I had convinced myself dishonesty about my spiritual life was better than genuine transparency.

Maybe you don't have to imagine a spiritual life that feels more like a burden than a blessing. Maybe you've experienced that burden in your past or you're carrying that burden now. If you've been there, you know keeping up a spiritual facade is hard work!

That period was draining for me. As I sat in Sunday morning worship services and examined the looks of calm confidence on people's faces as they worshiped or listened attentively to the preacher, I thought, *How do they all do it? How can they have it all together while I'm flailing and failing so miserably to live for Jesus?*

The weight of my religious burden was more than I could handle, and I wanted to give up.

## Bible Verses That Didn't Make Sense

One thing that confused me was how often I read Scripture verses that promised a different kind of life than the one I was experiencing. Some verses made absolutely no sense to me, and my honest heart response to them was, *What's up with that?*

For example, Jesus's words in Matthew 11:28–30 were a source of frustration. He said,

Come to Me, all who are weary and heavy-laden, and I will give you rest. Take My yoke upon you and learn from Me, for I am gentle and humble in heart, and you will find rest for your souls. For My yoke is easy and My burden is light.

Seriously? *Rest? Easy? Light?* Those words didn't describe my experience of following Jesus. If you had asked me to choose three words that *did* describe my Christian life, I would have chosen *work*, *hard*, and *heavy*. I was working hard to carry the heavy burden of living for Jesus.

*Am I doing all the right things? Am I not doing all the wrong things?* Those two questions constantly weighed me down. And the most frustrating part of the entire journey was that no matter how hard I tried, I always seemed to fail.

John 8:32 was another verse that made no sense to me. It's another statement from Jesus: "You will know the truth, and the truth will make you free."

Free? Are you kidding me? I didn't feel free. I felt like I was in bondage—bondage to a system of dos and don'ts, rules and regulations. And to make matters worse, by that point I had responded to God's call on my life to be a pastor, so to the best of my ability, I was trying to lead people along a journey of following Jesus I wasn't even sure existed.

**The Discovery That Changed My Life**

I spent many years trying to live for Jesus under the burden of religion. I even spent some of them as a seminary student and a senior pastor. But I'm grateful to say I don't carry that burden now. By God's grace, I've let go of religion and the pursuit of performing for Jesus, and I've embraced a life lived out of simply being with Jesus. I now enjoy the victory, moment by moment, of His life being lived through me.

How did this change come about? We'll discuss that process in detail throughout the pages of this book, but God finally set me free by using two crucial keys to unlock the bars of expectations that formed my spiritual prison.

The first key was my own spiritual brokenness. I eventually got to a place where I was broken down on many levels. God used a number of difficult circumstances to strip me of my desire to perform as a Christian. I was done trying to live the Christian life based on expectations, and after years of struggle, I'd finally reached a place of complete surrender.

The second key was an incredible mentor God brought into my life. His name was Clyde Cranford, and he helped me discover a spiritual truth that forever changed my life. This truth has formed the foundation of my spiritual life for decades now, and it serves as the foundation for what I want to communicate through this book: *the Christian life is not me living for Jesus but Jesus living His life in and through me.*

Let me unpack this idea in two chunks. First, *the Christian life is not me living for Jesus*, meaning, it's not all the religious "stuff" I've been talking about for the past few pages. It's not about the expectations, the dos and don'ts, the need to make it seem like I have it all together. None of that has any real connection to what it truly means to follow Jesus.

None of it.

Second is, *the Christian life is Jesus living His life in and through me*. Following Jesus has nothing to do with my ability or strength. It has everything to do with *His* ability and strength. That was the lesson I so desperately needed to learn—that Jesus never wanted me to push and strive my way into spiritual effectiveness. Instead,

He wanted me to pursue Him intimately, so in His own power, He could demonstrate His very life through me.

Believe me, what I'm talking about goes way beyond semantics. This isn't just another way of saying something; it's the difference between practicing a religion and pursuing a relationship.

Only one word can express what I felt when I finally grasped this reality: *freedom!* The burden of religion was removed, and I was free to follow Jesus with a simplicity and joy I'd never experienced.

That's what I want for you, and that's why I've written this book. I want to share the life-changing lessons I've learned. Specifically, I want to show you how three simple relationships can lead you to what Paul called "the simplicity and purity of devotion to Christ" (2 Cor. 11:3). Understanding the importance of those three relationships is absolutely essential for experiencing the abundant life Jesus promised, which is why they'll guide the structure of this book moving forward.

Those three relationships are the following:

1. Your relationship with God.
2. Your relationship with other believers.
3. Your relationship with the world.

You don't have to be burdened by the weight of living the Christian life based on performance and expectations. You can have the freedom and simplicity Jesus promises for every one of His followers.

Will you join me on this journey? I can't wait to get started!

# PART 1

# THE FOUNDATION

Everyone who hears these words of Mine and acts on them, may be compared to a wise man who built his house on the rock. And the rain fell, and the floods came, and the winds blew and slammed against that house; and yet it did not fall, for it had been founded on the rock.

Matthew 7:24–25

# 1

## The Problem

### *We're Aiming at the Wrong Target*

> The simplicity which is in Christ is rarely found among
> us. In its stead are programs, methods, organizations
> and a world of nervous activities which occupy time
> and attention but can never satisfy the longing of the
> heart.
>
> A. W. Tozer

If you were lucky enough to watch the 2004 Summer Olympic
Games in Athens, Greece, you probably remember swimmer Michael Phelps bursting onto the international scene. Phelps won six
medals in those games—four gold and two bronze—to launch his
career as the most decorated Olympic athlete in history.

But when I think back to those games, I think of Matt Emmons.

Emmons represented the United States in the three-position, fifty-meter rifle event, and he was dominating the competition as he advanced to the final shot of his signature event. His combined score was so far ahead of the other shooters that all he had to do was hit the target. I don't mean he had to hit the bull's-eye; he just had to hit anywhere on the entire target to secure a victory.

A sportswriter named Rick Reilly said it like this:

> With one shot to go in Athens, Emmons was on his way to a laugher of a win. . . . In fact, all he had to do was hit the target. It'd be like telling Picasso all he had to do was hit the canvas.[1]

In preparation for the shot, Emmons pressed his cheek against the rifle's stock and sighted down the barrel through the scope. He took a breath, let it out, and squeezed the trigger. The sound of the gun firing was unmistakable. What happened next was shocking.

When you watch the sport of rifle shooting, a monitor focused on the target is always on one of the corners of the TV screen. When a competitor takes a shot, that monitor almost immediately signals which part of the target was hit, and then a score is generated based on the quality of the shot.

When Emmons lowered his weapon, he immediately looked to see where his bullet had struck the target. But there was no mark. And there was no score. Confused, he began talking with the judges, indicating he believed he'd hit the target. Why was there no score?

Eventually, the lead judge picked up a microphone to explain. He announced that Emmons's score was zero because of a "cross shot." The crowd gasped! Emmons lowered his head, obviously unable to believe what had happened.

A cross shot is when a shooter hits a target that's not the one he's supposed to be shooting at. At some point while going through his pre-shot routine, Matt had zeroed in on the target *next* to his. His zero score not only lost him the gold medal; he fell out of medal contention completely.

Matt Emmons's story provides a great lesson: always be sure you're aiming at the right target.

### What's Your Target?

Let me ask you a couple of important questions about your life's target. First, do you desire to faithfully follow Jesus?

If you answered yes to that question, you've just identified the "target" of your life: to be a faithful Jesus follower. That's your bull's-eye. That's your aim—your primary goal.

Now, if that's your target, then your answer to the second question is extremely important. What does a faithful follower of Jesus look like? In other words, what are the characteristics of someone who hits that target? What does it look like to live that kind of life? Obviously, the answer is crucial—and finding the right answer can bring important clarity to our lives.

Before I share a few thoughts on the best way to answer that question, write your own answer in the space below. How would you describe what it means to be a faithful follower of Jesus?

Whether or not you realize it, you've been developing your spiritual target for what it means to be a "good Christian" for years—even before you first encountered God or desired to learn more about Him. If you grew up in a Christian home, for example, your parents were a major influence. The same is true of your experiences in church, the opinions of your friends, and the media you consumed.

The question, then, isn't whether you're aiming at a target when it comes to your spiritual life. You are. We all are. The question is whether you're aiming at the *right* target.

Sadly, I've seen many Christians aiming at the wrong target in their efforts to faithfully follow Jesus, creating heavy burdens that weigh them down and prevent them from experiencing the freedom and simplicity Jesus desires for us.

### Two Wrong Targets

When I look around the American church today, I see two primary targets people aim at in their spiritual lives: *activity* and *information*. Both of these targets are wrong when it comes to defining what it means to faithfully follow Jesus. Both lead to unnecessary burdens and a misrepresentation of Jesus to a watching world.

Making activity a target happens when we define following Jesus based on what we do. When we aim for this target, we make a list of all the activities "good Christians" are supposed to do to be considered faithful followers of Jesus. And then, of course, we also have to create a list of what "good Christians" are not supposed to do. (Since I've moved from Alabama to Las Vegas, I've noticed that the "not supposed to do" list can change a little—and sometimes it can change a lot.)

If the people around you define following Jesus this way, you'll hear statements like "Brother so-and-so is so faithful; he's at church every time the doors are open." Or "Sister so-and-so is so godly; she serves on thirty-two different ministry teams in our church, and she's on the waiting list for five more."

One of the reasons people drift toward this target is that it seems simple—maybe even easy. They think, *All I have to do is concentrate on doing the right things and not doing the wrong things. No problem!* But if you've ever tried to follow Jesus with this approach, you know how quickly those lists become a heavy burden.

Here's a sample of the list people have to maintain when they're aiming at a target based on activity:

- ☑ Attend church every week.
- ☑ Read your Bible every day.
- ☑ Pray every day.
- ☑ Consistently give a portion of your income to the church.
- ☑ Regularly share the gospel with others.
- ☑ Be a good husband/wife, father/mother, son/daughter.
- ☑ Work hard at your job.
- ☑ Don't gossip (unless it's disguised as a prayer request).
- ☑ Don't disrespect others.
- ☑ Don't break the Ten Commandments.

Now, maybe you looked over this list and thought, *Those all seem like good goals. What's the problem?* Let me be clear: nothing is wrong with these activities in and of themselves. Paul writes, "We are His workmanship, created in Christ Jesus for good works, which God prepared beforehand so that we would walk in them" (Eph. 2:10).

Doing good things and avoiding bad things isn't the problem. The problem is basing our lives on the false idea that doing good things and avoiding bad things earns some kind of spiritual credit in God's Heavenly Bank & Trust. It won't. We're just following a list of superficial, external traits that are nothing more than conformity to a system *we* created, not a system God created for us.

The second wrong target is information. This target defines following Jesus based on what a person knows. The focus is all about specific doctrines and spiritual knowledge. You know you're around people aiming at this target when you hear things like, "They seem nice, but don't they believe . . ." "Does he have the right doctrine? Can she recite all the creeds?" And of course, "Do they say it just like we say it?"

According to this way of thinking, to be a faithful follower of Jesus, you must

☑ Go to all the Bible studies, small groups, or Sunday school classes you can. (A seminary degree is preferred but not required.)

☑ Study the Bible for a couple of hours every day.

☑ Learn the right answers to all the difficult theological questions.

☑ Be able to recite the creeds and dogmas.

☑ Memorize enormous amounts of Scripture.

☑ Explain deep theological truths.

Once again, it's important to understand that there's nothing wrong with information on its own. Right doctrine is a crucial element of our faith, and it's helpful to know not only what we believe as Christians but why we believe it.

No, the problem with aiming at information as our spiritual target is that it elevates knowing about Jesus above knowing Jesus Himself.

Are you aiming at the wrong target in your spiritual life? If so, you're striving for standards that fall grossly short of the life Jesus modeled in the Gospels and the life He's invited us to experience throughout Scripture.

Trust me, I know from experience.

## My Story

I don't come from a long line of Christians. In fact, both my parents were the first people in their families to follow Christ, making that decision as high school students. By the time they married, my dad had accepted a call into the ministry, so my younger brother and I were both raised in the home of a Christian pastor.

I was always in and around church. That's just the way it goes for a pastor's family, and the church community was a major part of my life. But to be honest, that's as far as my spiritual development went as a kid. I knew the gospel well enough to answer all the questions I was expected to answer. I was even baptized. I still remember going under the water and then being pulled back up— dripping wet with my dad looking down at me—and wondering, *Did it work?*

I had no relationship with Jesus to speak of, at least not in any personal or meaningful way. At best, I had religion. I had things I was supposed to do, things I wasn't supposed to do, and stuff I was supposed to know.

As I got older, I became more and more aware of the lack of anything significant in my spiritual life. I had an emptiness inside me, but no matter how much I tried to do and say the right things, I couldn't shake it.

Throughout high school and into college, I searched for meaning and significance in other places. I tried sports, friends, popularity, dating, and partying—all the while maintaining my church life. Looking back, I can see I wasn't even basing my Christian life on doing the right things anymore; I just wanted others to think I was doing the right things.

Finally, as a freshman in college, I reached a breaking point. I knew I was one guy at church and a completely different guy on my college campus, and it was clear both guys were longing for something more. I was done with pretending I already had something I knew I needed. I was done with the whole system.

In desperation, I knelt beside my bed, alone in my college apartment. Tears streamed down my face as I cried out to God. And I did cry out to Him. I understood the gospel well enough to know Jesus was the only Person for me to turn to if I really wanted change. And I really wanted change.

In that moment, I surrendered my life to Jesus. I let go of control. I asked Him to take over, and He did. No glowing sunbeams shined down from heaven, and no angel choirs sang in the background, but I felt the change. I felt God's presence in a real and genuine way I'd never felt before.

I was so serious in that moment that I prayed, *God, if I ever turn back on this decision, please just take my life.* I had reached a point where I knew a relationship with Jesus was my only hope, and I had no desire to go back.

For the first time in my life, I felt at peace with God. I knew what it meant to be forgiven and to be accepted by Him. The morning after my conversion experience, I woke up and immediately opened my Bible—not because I had to but because I wanted to. I wanted to know this God who had just changed my life.

That was the good news. That was the encouraging part of my encountering a genuine faith in Jesus. The bad news was that I was still aiming at wrong targets. And the people I turned to for spiritual advice had the wrong targets in place as well. Even though I'd been changed on the inside and genuinely desired to be faithful as a follower of Jesus, I was still operating under the belief that being a good Christian meant doing the right things and avoiding the wrong things.

I paid more attention in church. I got connected with the accountability group I mentioned earlier. I memorized Scripture and journaled about my spiritual insights. I generally worked harder and concentrated deeper on doing all the things I had always believed good Christians were supposed to do. I even changed my career plans and began training toward full-time ministry.

In other words, I went back to religion. And as the months and years went by, I picked up all the weights and burdens of religious life that had dragged me down before—except this time I picked them up out of a sincere desire to be faithful as a follower of Jesus.

It wasn't until almost a decade later when, through the ministry and mentorship of Clyde Cranford, I was finally able to let those burdens go.

## Simplicity and Purity

What we know today as the book of 2 Corinthians is a letter written by the apostle Paul to his spiritual children in the ancient city of Corinth. During the time of the early church, Corinth was a wild place filled with immorality of all kinds. Not only that, but the church Paul had helped plant there was constantly under threat from internal struggles and strife. The Corinthians had information as their spiritual target, and they were bickering with one another, creating division in their efforts to settle on the "correct" set of doctrines that would lead them to be faithful followers of Jesus.

In the middle of that immorality and strife, Paul wrote 2 Corinthians as a spiritual parent concerned for his children. And in that letter, he used a phrase that strikes me as both profoundly wise and incredibly relevant for Christians in our culture.

He said, "I am afraid that, as the serpent deceived Eve by his craftiness, your minds will be led astray from the simplicity and purity of devotion to Christ" (2 Cor. 11:3). Think about that wording for a moment: *the simplicity and purity of devotion to Christ.*

Do the words *simple* and *pure* describe your relationship with Jesus? They didn't for me. Not for a long time. And they don't for a large percentage of Christians today.

Why is that?

The answer is that we often prefer a superficial system of religion over a genuine relationship with Christ because the superficial system is easier to control. We have a built-in desire to measure our performance whenever possible—not because we want to excel but because it makes it easy for us to say, "I may not be perfect, but I'm doing much better than *those* people."

When Jesus confronted the Pharisees during the last week before His crucifixion, He put His finger directly on this tendency in our lives:

> Jesus spoke to the crowds and to His disciples, saying: "The scribes and the Pharisees have seated themselves in the chair of Moses; therefore all that they tell you, do and observe, but do not do according to their deeds; for they say things and do not do them. They tie up heavy burdens and lay them on men's shoulders, but

they themselves are unwilling to move them with so much as a finger. (Matt. 23:1–4)

Religion is one of those "heavy burdens." And like the Pharisees, those of us in the modern church are in danger of allowing a bunch of superficial rules, traditions, and dogmas to distract us from what it really means to follow Jesus. We've substituted all these things for the simplicity and purity of devotion to Him. And in doing so, tragically, we've aimed at the wrong target. That's a big problem.

Thankfully, there's a solution.

# 2

## The Solution

### *It's All about Relationships*

> The Christian life is nothing less than the life which
> He lived then . . . lived *now* by Him in *you*.
>
> Major Ian Thomas

In May 2018, in a Connecticut hospital, a group of twelve surgeons worked for five hours to remove a tumor from the abdomen of a thirty-eight-year-old woman. That may seem like a lot of doctors and a long time for a single tumor—until you learn that single tumor weighed 132 pounds!

The patient reported that, prior to the surgery, the tumor had grown at a rate of ten pounds per week. That's forty pounds a month!

"Ovarian mucinous tumors tend to be big," said Dr. Vaagn Andikyan, who was the lead surgeon on the team. "But tumors this big are exceedingly rare in the literature. It may be in the top 10 or 20 tumors of this size removed worldwide." The tumor was technically benign, but it was far from harmless. According to Dr. Andikyan, the patient couldn't walk, she was malnourished because she'd been unable to eat, and she was at extreme danger for blood clots and other blood-vessel-related damage. Her very life was in jeopardy.

"When I first walked into the examination room . . . I saw fear in the patient's eyes," Dr. Andikyan said. "She was so hopeless, because she had seen several other doctors, and they were unable to help her."

Can you imagine trying to go about your day with a 132-pound weight dragging you down *from the inside*? Can you imagine the pressure that must have built up in and around that poor woman—the squeezing, maddening, crushing pressure?

But then can you imagine what that patient must have felt like the day after the surgery? The week after? Can you imagine the change that must have taken place after a 132-pound burden was removed? "She's back to a normal life, she's back to work," the doctor said. "And when I saw her in my office, I saw smiles, I saw hope, and I saw a happy woman who is back to her normal life and her family."[1]

Wouldn't you like to experience that kind of joy? That kind of freedom?

I have. And believe me, it's as wonderful as it sounds.

**My Mentor**

I've never had a 132-pound tumor removed from my body, but as I described in the previous chapter, I did spend years trying to live for Jesus under the crushing burden of religion—of always having to do the right thing, know the right thing, and maintain the standard of everyone else's expectations because I was aiming at the wrong spiritual target.

And just like that poor woman in Connecticut, I felt as if I'd tried everything to find answers with no results. My burden kept growing week after week, month after month, year after year.

Then I met Clyde Cranford. He was my spiritual surgeon—although it took him a lot longer than five hours to help me find freedom.

I first met Clyde while I was attending seminary. He'd graduated from the same school many years earlier, and occasionally he returned to campus to lead worship in our chapel service. Clyde's ministry, Life to Life Ministries, was a one-on-one discipleship program focused on training men in ministry.

Clyde was one of those people often described as "unique." Physically, nothing made him stand out from the crowd. He was average in height and appearance. His skin had a pasty look that made it seem like he rarely went outside. He wasn't athletic at all, and during the years I knew him, he struggled with thyroid issues and medications that left him overweight.

Because of the ministry path he'd chosen, Clyde didn't have much in terms of money or prestige. I never went shopping with him, but I'm pretty sure most of his wardrobe came from thrift stores—his clothes never seemed to fit quite right.

What I'm saying is Clyde's physical appearance and persona didn't attract others to his presence. What made him so special was who he was spiritually. When he walked into a room, it was as if the glory of God came in through the door right with him. You could just tell he knew what it meant to be with Jesus.

I was going through a period of real spiritual brokenness when I first began interacting with Clyde. He heard about it and reached out to ask if I would be interested in meeting with him on a regular basis. I immediately said yes! I was at such a point of brokenness that I was desperate for help.

Over the next couple of years, I met with Clyde for about two hours every Thursday afternoon. That time with him changed my life—there's no other way to say it.

As I mentioned in the introduction, Clyde showed me that the Christian life isn't about me living for Jesus but Jesus living His life in and through me. That truth alone was an incredible gift. But Clyde didn't stop there; he didn't just point me toward a better target. He also showed me how to change. He helped me let go of religion and embrace the immeasurable blessing of simply enjoying a relationship that would allow Jesus to accomplish His purpose through me.

That's the same blessing—the same gift—I want for you as we journey through this process together. And if the Christian life is really Jesus living His life through me, the next step on this journey is to understand that Jesus's life on earth revolved around three primary relationships.

## The Three Relationships

On December 23, 2000, my family arrived in Las Vegas. My wife and I felt strongly that God had called us to plant a new community of believers in that city, and we were excited to join what He was already doing. That's how Hope Church was born.

For the first year of our ministry, the leadership team at Hope Church wrestled with this question: What does a faithful follower of Jesus look like? We wanted a goal not only for ourselves but to serve as a foundation for spiritual growth within our new community of Jesus followers.

After a full year of intense prayer and study, we made a discovery that still strikes me as so amazing and yet so wonderfully simple. We realized that Jesus's life revolved around three specific relationships. And we also concluded that if we were going to allow His life to be lived in and through us, our lives would need to be built around the same three relationships.

Imagine you're sitting at your kitchen table. In front of you are a Bible, three empty boxes, and a pair of scissors—good, sharp scissors that can do some precision work. Now imagine opening the Bible to the Gospels and physically cutting out every story recorded in Matthew, Mark, Luke, and John.

If you then arrange each story by category, you'll discover that every one of them could easily fit into one of those three empty boxes, each box representing one of the primary relationships in Jesus's life.

### Box 1: Jesus's Relationship with His Father

The Gospels are filled with stories about Jesus and His relationship with God the Father. In Matthew, the Father signaled His approval of the Son at Jesus's baptism. "While he was still speaking, a bright cloud overshadowed them, and behold, a voice out of the cloud said, 'This is My beloved Son, with whom I am well-pleased; listen to Him!'" (17:5). In Mark, Jesus's glory was revealed in the Father's presence on the Mount of Transfiguration (9:1–8). In Luke, we read about Jesus spending an entire night in prayerful communion with the Father before choosing His disciples (6:12–16). And when we read John 17, we're allowed to peer into a moment of spiritual intimacy between the Father and the Son in the garden of Gethsemane on the night before Jesus's crucifixion.

When I read these stories and so many more throughout the Gospels, it's clear to me that Jesus prioritized spending time with the Father above all else. And it's important for us to understand that everything Jesus accomplished flowed from His intimate fellowship with the Father. When the people of Jesus's day saw Him perform some great miracle, that was because the Father was working in and through Him. When they heard Jesus speak, that was the Father speaking through His Son. Everything about Jesus's life was produced by the power of the Holy Spirit, born from His intimacy with the Father and overflowed into the world.

Jesus Himself made that clear: "Do you not believe that I am in the Father, and the Father is in Me? The words that I say to you I do not speak on My own initiative, but the Father abiding in Me does His works. Believe Me that I am in the Father and the Father is in Me" (John 14:10–11).

Jesus also made these astonishing claims during His ministry:

- "Truly, truly, I say to you, the Son can do nothing of Himself, unless it is something He sees the Father doing; for whatever the Father does, these things the Son also does in like manner" (John 5:19).
- "When you lift up the Son of Man, then you will know that I am He, and I do nothing on My own initiative, but I speak these things as the Father taught Me. And He who sent Me is with Me; He has not left Me alone, for I always do the things that are pleasing to Him" (John 8:28–29).

Both these Scriptures are examples of passages we sometimes breeze through without really catching the radical nature of what's being said. But look at that word Jesus used both times: *nothing*.

Did you hear that? When Jesus described His ability apart from the Father, He chose the word *nothing*. Twice.

Jesus modeled what it looks like to live in total dependence on the Holy Spirit through moment-by-moment fellowship with the Father. Now, don't misunderstand me when I use that word *modeled*. Jesus is infinitely more than a model. He is God in human flesh, who atoned for the sins of the world. But that doesn't diminish the reality that, in His humanity, He also modeled what it looks like to live in complete dependence on the Spirit through intimacy with the Father.

What's more, we can see Jesus diligently maintaining that connection in the Gospels. He often slipped away into the wilderness to spend time with the Father, just the two of them. Many times, He stopped to settle in a garden or go up a mountain to be alone with God.

How much more should this be true of us? If we want to faithfully follow Jesus, we need to daily cultivate a vital relationship with our Father, as did Jesus.

### Box 2: Jesus's Relationship with the Disciples

The second box on your kitchen table is filled with the many Gospel stories about Jesus actively and intentionally cultivating relationships with His disciples.

He started by calling them away from their old lives so they could join in His kingdom activity. Then Jesus prayed with His disciples. He taught them, cared for them, challenged them, and walked with each of them through the ups and downs of life.

In Matthew, we see Jesus healing Peter's mother-in-law (8:14–15). In Mark, Jesus joined the disciples on what was supposed to be a quick sail across the Sea of Galilee—and He used the resulting storm to teach them about the power of faith in difficult times (4:35–41). In Luke, Jesus challenged His disciples to feed a crowd of more than five thousand people, and then He challenged them to trust God in every circumstance by using only five loaves and two fish to provide a feast for them all (9:12–27). And in John, we read with amazement that Jesus, for all His miracles and power and glory, gave His disciples an incredible picture of servant leadership by kneeling in front of each one and washing their feet (13:5–20).

The Gospels were written by four of Jesus's followers, and they serve as historical records of the relationship and fellowship that existed between the Lord and His friends. Jesus poured His life into the disciples. He lived His life in an intimate, personal relationship with the Father that spilled into an intentional relationship of fellowship with them.

### Box 3: Jesus's Relationship with the World

That final box on your kitchen table is filled with stories about Jesus and His relationship with the world—meaning, with those who didn't know God and weren't part of His kingdom. When you journey through the Gospels, you read story after story of Jesus seeking out people who were in desperate need of His saving grace.

In Matthew, we see the religious leaders accusing Him of being a friend of sinners because He joined the hated tax collectors for a meal (9:9–13). In Mark, Jesus is compelled to connect with those whose lives have been wrecked by demonic strongholds so he can set them free. In Luke, He's welcomed into the home of a tax collector named Zacchaeus (19:1–10). And in John, Jesus is constantly looking to engage with those who are far from God to bring to them the life-changing message of the gospel—whether it's those lost in the darkness of religion, like Nicodemus, or those trapped in the seduction of sexual sin, like the Samaritan woman.

One of the key patterns in Jesus's life was building intentional, engaging, loving relationships with people who were far from God so they could come to know God through Him. May the same be said of our lives!

I encourage you to keep this illustration of three boxes, a Bible, and a pair of scissors in mind as you read through the Gospels. Test this for yourself. You'll see that every page has a description of Jesus's relationship with the Father, with the disciples, or with the world. As we say at Hope Church, the life of Jesus is all about relationships! That's the life Jesus lived during His ministry on earth.

But where does Jesus live now? Most people would probably say "heaven" right off the bat, and that's certainly true. But that's not the whole answer.

Right now, this very minute, Jesus lives in me. And if you've accepted the call to follow Him, He also lives in you. By the indwelling of His Spirit, He has taken up residence in our lives. And He desires to live through us.

It's worth saying again: the Christian life is not you and me trying to do good things and avoid bad things. The Christian life is not even you and me trying to mimic the life Jesus lived. Those approaches create burdens. The Christian life is the life of Jesus Christ fleshed out in our lives—yours and mine—through the power of the Holy Spirit.

And as we allow Jesus to live His life through us by the power of His Spirit, here's what it looks like: those same three relationships.

### Abide, Connect, Share

I promised I would guide you through the process of removing the burden of religion from your spiritual life and help you aim at the best possible target for a faithful follower of Jesus. Just as God transformed my life all those years ago through Clyde Cranford, I pray that after we've completed our journey together through this book, He'll have transformed your life too—through discovering the freedom and simplicity of following Jesus.

The three relationships I've just described are the scaffolding for the process of removing the burden of religion. They provide the structure. But I want to connect a specific word to each of them to simplify terminology: *Abide*, *Connect*, and *Share*.

### *Abide*

The word *Abide* is designed to help you remember that following Jesus is first and foremost about your relationship with Him. It's about that wonderful, intimate fellowship between you and your Savior. And if you think that sounds kind of simple, you're right! It's supposed to be simple.

The sad truth is that we in the church have been overcomplicating what it means to follow Jesus for centuries. We've burdened ourselves with rituals and traditions that go way beyond what Jesus asked of His early disciples and what He asks of us. Worse, we've burdened ourselves with religious expectations that pull us away from Jesus rather than allowing us to enjoy time with Him.

What we've made complicated, Jesus made simple in the Gospels. He even summarized the whole thing by simply walking into a vineyard and picking up a branch that had broken loose from a grapevine:

Abide in Me, and I in you. As the branch cannot bear fruit of itself unless it abides in the vine, so neither can you unless you abide in Me. I am the vine, you are the branches; he who abides in Me and I in him, he bears much fruit, for apart from Me you can do nothing. (John 15:4–5)

Simplicity. Jesus summed up the whole dynamic of being His disciple with one little word: *Abide.*

What good is a branch without the vine? It's no good at all, right? If you break the branch off a vine, the branch is useless by itself. It can't do anything. (Unless you're a little kid who needs to make a sword.) In truth, the only thing the branch is good for is holding on to the vine. And only in holding on to the vine does the branch produce fruit.

That creates another question. What is fruit, and is it the result of a branch's hard work? No. Fruit is the life of the vine pressed out through the branches. If the vine is a grapevine, the fruit pressed out of the branches are grapes. With an apple tree, the fruit pressed out of its branches are apples. Again, simple!

In Jesus's illustration, who is the vine? Jesus. Who's the branch? We are. And our spiritual fruit is the life of Jesus in us being lived through us as we abide in Him. The invitation to follow Jesus isn't an invitation to live for Jesus; it's an invitation to abide in Jesus and let Him, out of the overflow of that relationship, live His life in and through us in a way that produces fruit for His kingdom.

Are you abiding in Christ? Is your experience of following Jesus all about abiding in Him? Are you following Jesus in a moment-by-moment love relationship that's the center and source of everything else in your life? Or have you relegated following Jesus to a few hours of activity each week?

As a Jesus follower, your identity is not in what you do. Your identity is in who you are in Christ—a loved, accepted child of the Father enjoying a fellowship relationship with Him. Great freedom is in understanding and enjoying the difference!

### Connect

The foundation of following Jesus, then, is a vibrant, loving relationship with God. And when I take time to abide in Christ, my relationship with God spills into a second relationship that's also crucial to my spiritual life: my relationship with other believers. Just as Jesus had an intimate love relationship with the Father and a relationship with His disciples, we have an intimate love relationship with God that brings us into relationships with our brothers and sisters in Christ.

It's important to understand that this second relationship didn't start with the church; it's not a "New Testament" relationship. We were made for relationships from the beginning of creation.

The Bible opens with the incredible story of the world's origins. On day one God made light and said, "It is good." On day two He made the sky and said, "It is good." On day three God made the land, water, plants, and trees and said, "It is good." On day four He made the sun, moon, and stars, and He said yet again, "It is good." On day five God made the birds and the fish, and He said, "It is good." On day six He made all the animals and said, "It is good."

That's when the pattern stopped. In Genesis 2, we read these words: "Then the Lord God formed man of dust from the ground, and breathed into his nostrils the breath of life; and man became a living being. . . . Then the Lord God said, 'It is not good for the man to be alone'" (vv. 7, 18).

What wasn't good?

Up until that point, everything had been good. What about God's creation of humanity was not good? God said it was not good for man to be alone. Meaning, God didn't create human beings to know Him and love Him in isolation from relationships with others. His design was for our relationship with Him to be enjoyed in the context of relationship with other people.

Some people in today's culture like to argue about this idea, saying, "My relationship with God is personal." That's true. We do have a personal relationship with God. But it was never designed to be private. It's a relationship He's given us to be lived out in the context of community. And for those of us who've given our lives to following Jesus, that community is called the church.

On the other side of the coin, some people say, "I must attend church to be a good Christian." No! We don't attend church because we must to gain God's approval. Church is the community God, in His sovereignty, established as a place of connection. A place where brothers and sisters in Christ can come together and enjoy fellowship with one another. I don't "have to" attend church to make God happy. I "get to" attend church to deepen my relationship with Him through community with others.

This dynamic expression of community is exactly what the first disciples experienced when the church was born. In Acts 2, thousands of people became Jesus followers on the same day, and they immediately began living out their relationship with God in fellowship with one another.

This fellowship took place in two environments, as we see in Acts 2:46:

1. Large groups—"day by day continuing with one mind in the temple"
2. Small groups—"breaking bread from house to house"

The apostles taught the Word of God in the temple courts, and the community of believers worshiped together around that Word. Then, as they gathered house to house in small groups, they reviewed the apostles' teaching and applied it to their lives as they prayed and shared life together.

The early Christians didn't invent that approach either. They were following the model Jesus lived out during His ministry. At times, Jesus taught large numbers of people—even multitudes. Other times, He pulled away and gathered with a smaller group of disciples to help them apply those truths to their personal lives.

That's exactly why most churches attempt to establish large-group gatherings for worship and small-group gatherings for mutual care, fellowship, and sharing life together. This isn't just a program invented by churches; it's the paradigm Jesus modeled for us in the New Testament and the practice lived out by those first believers in the early church.

The key word for this second relationship is *Connect*. As followers of Jesus, we're to connect with other believers. If your experience of Christianity is trying to enjoy your relationship with God in isolation, I have two Bible words for you: *not good!* As the writer of Ecclesiastes said, "Woe to the one who falls when there is not another to lift him up" (4:10).

In the first eleven verses of John 15, Jesus describes the simplicity of abiding in Him—reminding us that He is the vine and we are the branches. But then in verse 12, He gives an example of what it looks like when our abiding in Him overflows into the rest of our lives. He says, "This is My commandment, that you love one another." If that was all He said, that alone would be a significant statement. But then He adds, "just as I have loved you."

Don't miss that second part. Jesus was teaching us that the first defining mark of abiding in Him and living out of the overflow of intimacy with God is developing a loving, fellowship relationship with our brothers and sisters in Christ. Let that sink in. Going to a Sunday service and offering a few casual greetings isn't living out this principle. Jesus set a much higher standard: "Just as I have loved you." You must be actively involved in the lives of others to live this out.

Now, I'm not saying you have to go to church and join a small group to be a good Christian. We're not going back to religion. I'm saying following Jesus is a love relationship with the Father that spills into fellowship with other followers of Christ. If you're faithfully following Jesus, that's what your life will reflect.

### Share

Finally, following Jesus is about a relationship with the world. Not only did Jesus have a love relationship with the Father that spilled into a fellowship relationship with His disciples, but those connections also overflowed into relationships with people who didn't know God at all. The same should be true for us.

In John 17:18, Jesus said, "As You [the Father] sent Me into the world, I also have sent them into the world." Can I let you in on a secret? You're the "them" in this verse. And because you're the "them," you need to understand that Jesus said the Father sent Him into the world on mission and now He's sent us into the world on that same mission.

Do you realize what that means? Evangelism—what we often call "sharing the gospel"—isn't just for those we officially call evangelists. Mission trips and missionary work aren't activities specially designed for the Navy SEALs of the church. Those expressions of our faith aren't reserved for the spiritually elite. They're the life of Jesus in us being lived through us. Because it's who He is, it's who we are as His followers.

If that kind of relationship with the world isn't evident in your life, you're missing the target. Jesus came to restore humanity's relationship with God, to make it right again. The Bible word for this is *reconciliation*. Humanity was separated from God because of sin, but then Jesus came to bring reconciliation.

This is how Paul describes this concept in 2 Corinthians 5:18–20:

> Now all these things are from God, who reconciled us to Himself through Christ and gave us the ministry of reconciliation, namely, that God was in Christ reconciling the world to Himself, not counting their trespasses against them, and He has committed to us the word of reconciliation.
>
> Therefore, we are ambassadors for Christ, as though God were making an appeal through us; we beg you on behalf of Christ, be reconciled to God.

Did you notice how the apostle Paul refers to you as a follower of Jesus? You are an ambassador for Christ. He doesn't say you *will be* an ambassador. He doesn't even ask if you want to be an ambassador. He says you *are* an ambassador. And it's the role of an ambassador to actively and intentionally make connections with others in the world.

Sharing in God's mission and telling others the good news about Jesus aren't programs of the church you can opt into or out of. They're simply evidence of the life of Christ being manifested in your life out of the overflow of intimacy with God. If there's a deficiency in your life in the area of sharing the gospel with others, it ultimately reveals a deficiency in your personal love relationship with Jesus. If you're not passionate about the nations hearing the message of Jesus, then that reveals an area of your heart that doesn't reflect the heart of Jesus.

When you're abiding in Christ, His life is evident in your life, and what's on His heart will be on your heart. And as we examine the Gospels, we see those who are far from God were clearly on the heart of Jesus.

The key word for this third relationship is *Share*. We are to share in God's mission both locally and globally. Just as Christ came into the world on mission from the Father, He has now sent us into the world on mission. For that reason, mission isn't what we *do* as Jesus followers; being on mission is who we *are* as Jesus followers.

A glorious gathering will be around the throne of Jesus one day, and the Bible says it will represent every tribe, every tongue, every people, and every nation—all worshiping, exalting, and praising the name of Jesus. It's kind of like the opening ceremony for eternity. Here's what I'm saying to you today: every moment of our lives is to be lived on mission in light of that moment around the throne of Jesus. I'm not living for a great career or a comfortable retirement. I'm living for that moment when, around the throne of Jesus, people from every culture and of every color will exalt His name together.

As a faithful follower of Jesus, that is my mission.

### It Takes All Three

*Abide*, *Connect*, and *Share*. These words represent three relationships that are interdependent. Listen to the way Jesus describes this in John 13:34–35: "A new commandment I give to you, that you love one another, even as I have loved you [Abide], that you also love one another [Connect]. By this all men will know [Share] that you are My disciples, if you have love for one another."

Do you see how He powerfully wove all three relationships together? It's out of the overflow of our love relationship with Him that God manifests through us the kind of love He desires us to have for one another. Then those relationships become the greatest platform we have to authenticate the gospel to this world. It takes all three to faithfully follow Jesus.

According to renowned Greek scholar Spiros Zodhiates, the Greek word from which we get our English word *disciple* means "not only to learn, but to become attached to one's teacher and to become his follower in doctrine and conduct of life."[2] In Jesus's day, the defining mark of disciples was the relationship they enjoyed with the one they were following. The same is true in our day.

Being a disciple of Jesus isn't just conforming to a system of moral behavior, nor is it merely comprehending a set of doctrinal truths. Following Jesus is first and foremost a relationship. It's all about relationships!

Are you ready to take the next step on this journey toward letting go of the burden of religion? These three words—*Abide*, *Connect*, and *Share*—will serve as the key landmarks on your path. Are you ready to aim at the best possible target as a follower of Jesus? You'll hit it as you Abide in Christ, Connect in community, and Share in God's mission for the world.

# PART 2

# ABIDE

I am the true vine, and My Father is the vine-dresser. Every branch in Me that does not bear fruit, He takes away; and every branch that bears fruit, He prunes it so that it may bear more fruit. You are already clean because of the word which I have spoken to you. Abide in Me, and I in you. As the branch cannot bear fruit of itself unless it abides in the vine, so neither can you unless you abide in Me.

John 15:1–4

# 3

# The Goal of the Christian Life

God must do everything for us. Our part is to yield
and trust.

A. W. Tozer

While growing up in Brooklyn in the 1960s, Ashrita Furman was
fascinated by the *Guinness World Records* book. Every year, he'd eagerly buy the newest edition to find out which crazy new records had
been created and which of his favorite old records had been broken.

Furman set a goal to achieve his own world record one day, and he
achieved that goal in 1979. That was the year he performed jumping
jacks for six hours and forty-five minutes straight, setting the record
for the most consecutive jumping jacks at twenty-seven thousand.

For most people, achieving a childhood goal like that would
bring some satisfaction, maybe even a moment of triumph, and
that would be the end of the story. But Ashrita Furman is not most
people. The thrill of setting a world record sparked a desire for
more, and he's set records ever since.

Here are just a few of the world records Furman has set over the past thirty years:

- The greatest distance traveled while somersaulting: 12 miles, 390 yards
- The most weight balanced in a milk crate on a person's chin: 93 pounds, 7 ounces
- The largest Hula-Hoop spun around a human body a minimum of three times: 16 feet, 6.7 inches
- The most apples cut in midair with a samurai sword in under one minute: 29
- The greatest distance traveled while juggling on a pogo stick: 4 miles, 30 feet[1]

Amazingly, Furman has set more than six hundred world records over his lifetime—including the world record for holding the most world records!

When asked if any record would finally make him feel satisfied, Furman said, "I don't feel like there's any one thing that's going to give me satisfaction—like, 'That one I have to do and I'll be satisfied.' I always want to be, you know, transcending. I always want to be going after a new goal."[2]

In that sense, Ashrita is almost a walking personification of our culture's obsession with goals and achievements. But that obsession doesn't serve us well when it comes to living as a faithful follower of Jesus.

## Not Doing but Being

In America and throughout much of the West, society is extremely goal oriented. We have goals for everything: goals for exercise and diet with our bodies, goals for finances and education within our families, goals for revenue and market share within our businesses. We expend a great deal of effort toward achieving these accomplishments.

In light of that obsession, have you ever wondered about the goals of the Christian life? We know our ultimate target is to live as faithful followers of Jesus, but what goals can we set and achieve to help us get there?

Some people would immediately respond to that question with "The goal of the Christian life is to live for God!" They would say God has done so much for them that the least they can do is try to live for Him to the best of their ability. With this mind-set, though, the goal of the Christian life can be summed up in one word: *obedience*. Meaning this: *the more I live for God through obedience, the closer I get to hitting the target of being a good Christian.*

If this is your mind-set, you have a problem. Building your life around the goal of obeying God is a step back toward religion, not relationship. It's just another burden—another weight around your neck.

In addition, living in total obedience to God is absolutely impossible in our own strength on this side of eternity. We can't do it, and we know we can't do it. Unfortunately, pursuing a goal we know we can't achieve leads to guilt and condemnation. We know we can't measure up, and so we take on another burden.

Thankfully, Jesus gave a clear picture of His goal for His disciples all the way back at the beginning of His public ministry: "He went up on the mountain and summoned those whom He Himself wanted, and they came to Him. And He appointed twelve, so that they would be with Him and that He could send them out to preach" (Mark 3:13–14).

Earlier, Jesus had called specific individuals to follow Him as He traveled to different regions around Galilee, including when

He promised to make Simon Peter and Andrew "fishers of men" (Mark 1:17) and when He commanded Levi the tax collector, "Follow Me!" (2:14). But here in Mark 3, Jesus had gathered all His would-be disciples on a mountain retreat. And from among them, He chose twelve men and personally invited them to walk with Him, live with Him, and teach with Him as disciples. Today, these men are known as the apostles.

With that in mind, look again at Mark 3:14: "He appointed twelve, so that they would be with Him and that He could send them out to preach." Why did Jesus call these men as disciples? *So they would be with Him.* Jesus didn't say their purpose was to live for Him. He didn't say He was calling them to obey Him or honor Him or please Him in some way. He called them so they could be with Him and He could be with them.

Don't miss this truth: this Scripture clearly teaches that following Jesus is not about doing; it's about being.

Of course, verse 14 has a second part: "And . . . He could send them out to preach." I know someone out there is thinking, *Aha! I knew we would get to the "doing" part. It says Jesus sent them out to preach. Isn't that what they had to do?*

Jesus did send the disciples out to preach. But notice the "they" and the "He" in that verse. "They" were to be with Him. "He" would send them out to preach. The Greek word translated "preach" means to announce publicly or to make public. "They," the disciples, were first called to be with Jesus. And then, out of the overflow of their being with Him, "He" would make His life public through them. Jesus would accomplish His mission through the disciples as an overflow of their spending time with Him.

We need to understand that being with Jesus is the ultimate pursuit of our lives. *Being* with Jesus always comes before *doing* anything. Doing flows from being, not the other way around.

This is a crucial principle for anyone who wants to live as a faithful follower of Jesus: *the primary call on my life is not to do something for Jesus; the primary call on my life is to be with Jesus.*

When I caught the truth of this principle under the mentorship of Clyde Cranford, I was blown away. For the first time, I realized that Jesus didn't invite me into a relationship with Him so I could do something for Him. He called me to Himself so I could be with Him. The simplicity of this truth allowed me to finally experience real freedom after years of trying to live "for" Jesus. I found freedom from rules and regulations, freedom from dos and don'ts—freedom to simply be with Jesus.

## What's Our Goal?

Let's get back to the central question for this chapter: What is the Christian life? The target is to faithfully follow Jesus, but how do we get there?

The simple answer is wrapped up in our key word for this part of our journey: *Abide.* Remember, following Jesus is all about relationships, and that first relationship revolves around abiding in Him to enjoy the wonderful gift of a personal relationship with God.

Now, what does this principle of Abide look like on a practical level? Think about the goal of being with Jesus through the filter of two primary objectives.

### 1. The Overall Objective: To Know God

The overall objective is to know God personally. And yes, you really can know God.

One of the big misconceptions or straight-out false teachings within our culture is that God exists as some kind of "force" or abstract being. Even when people in our culture profess a belief in God as a divine Creator, they often think of Him as distant and abstract—as if He were some cosmic being who created everything and then wandered off into space.

That's not God. The God who revealed Himself to us in the Bible is a Person. And in Genesis 1, Scripture makes it clear that God created human beings not as separate from Him but in His own image. That's key, because being created in God's image means we can relate with Him. We can know Him even as we are known by Him.

I love the way Jesus expressed this concept in John 17:3: "This is eternal life, that they may know You, the only true God, and Jesus Christ whom You have sent." Did you know eternal life doesn't start when we get to heaven? For followers of Jesus, eternal life is happening right now, right here on earth. Eternal life is the incredible gift and privilege of personally knowing the only true God.

As I mentioned above, it is possible to know God. And it's important to understand that the word *know* is an important term in the Greek language. It doesn't mean to know *about* something. You and I know about many people; we know about political figures, sports heroes, and celebrities. But we probably don't know them personally. In John 17:3, the word *know* implies direct, personal fellowship. It describes relationship. It speaks to intimacy.

Now, all this leads to a difficult question: Why don't we know God better? There's a good answer, and it has everything to do with this concept of Abide.

On May 23, 1992, I stood in front of a congregation that included my family and closest friends. I was all dressed up in a tuxedo, but best of all, my bride, Kristie, stood by my side in her wedding dress. I think I looked okay, but she looked amazing! On that day, before the Lord and all those people, I declared, "Kristie, I love you." And on May 23, 1992, I meant that with all my heart.

But today I love her even more than I could have loved her in 1992. Why? Because today I know her in a way I didn't know her back then. And the more I've grown to know her, the more I've grown to love her. Knowing her more intimately has caused me to love her more deeply.

Now, imagine me standing on that stage in my tuxedo. I've got a goofy grin on my face, and I'm turned toward Kristie to make my vows to her. Imagine what would happen if I said the following:

> Kristie, today I'm pledging to be your husband, and here's how it's going to look. Every Sunday morning, I'll come see you for an hour or two—unless a ball game is on or the weather is bad or I just feel like sleeping in. But other than all that, you can count on me to be there every week.
>
> And, Kristie, I love you so much that, one night a week, I'll have a group of people over to my house, and we'll invite you to come as well.
>
> Now, we're not going to spend much more time than that together unless I need something. If I do, I'll call you. And I'll not only call you; I'll have all my friends call you. And by the way, when I tell you I need something, I'll need it right away.

How do you think my bride would respond? No woman in her right mind would accept a vow like that! (And no man in his right mind would make a vow like that within arm's reach of that woman.) Why would that scenario be a problem? Because it looks nothing like a loving relationship. You could never really know another person given that kind of routine.

Do you see where I'm headed? So often we say, *God, I want to give You my life; I want You to be the center of it! So I'm going to show up on Sunday for an hour or two.* And then we wonder why we struggle with this thing called the Christian life.

We struggle because we can't develop a relationship with someone we don't know. We can't put God in a box that gets opened only twice a week and expect to live the victorious, abundant life He describes in His Word.

That brings us to the second primary objective in discovering what it means practically to abide in Christ.

### 2. The Daily Objective: To Spend Time with God

If we want a genuine relationship with God, we have to get to know Him. And if we want to get to know Him, we need to spend time with Him each day. It's not rocket science. I know many people want to make Christianity overly complicated and theologically deep, but that's never been what God intended. The Christian life is wonderfully simple and pure when we truly understand the importance of abiding in Christ.

When we look at the New Testament, we see Jesus's disciples making a lot of mistakes. So many times, they totally missed what Jesus was trying to teach them. So many moments, they reacted inappropriately, failed to trust Jesus, or even worked against His plans.

But the disciples did at least one major thing right: they spent time with Jesus. Every day. When Jesus performed a miracle, the disciples were there to see it and be amazed. When Jesus taught in the synagogues, the disciples were there to hear and learn. And when Jesus hiked from town to town and region to region to spread the gospel, the disciples hiked with Him and helped Him share the good news.

That's how the disciples were able to launch and lead a movement that changed the course of human history. Not because of what they knew or did but because they spent years being with Jesus.

That raises another challenging question: Why don't we spend more time with Jesus?

Because I've been a pastor for decades, I've spent a lot of time with people seeking to live the Christian life. I often ask them, "What's the most difficult thing for you to consistently practice in your spiritual life?" Without a doubt, the response I hear far more often than any other is "Spending time alone with God every day." Why is that?

Because we have two enemies.

Our first enemy is on the outside. It's Satan (and to a lesser extent, the world in which we live). Make no mistake, if you're seeking to faithfully follow Jesus, you have an enemy who hates everything about God and God's kingdom, and he'll try to block, prevent, or hinder you from abiding in Christ.

Your enemy knows the Christian life is all about relationships, and so he doesn't care what you *do* as long as you don't take the time to *be* with God. If you busy yourself with hours and hours of spiritual activity, he'll leave you alone. But if you try to make spiritual intimacy with God a priority, he'll bombard you with distraction after distraction.

Jim Elliot, a great missionary who sacrificed his life taking the gospel to unreached peoples, summarized it this way: "I think the devil has made it his business to monopolize on three elements: noise, hurry, crowds. . . . Satan is quite aware of the power of silence."[3]

But another enemy often hinders or even completely blocks our efforts to spend time with God too. That enemy is within. It's us. It's our own wants and wishes and desires and dreams. What we think is important to accomplish each day often doesn't leave room for spending time with God. In other words, we don't spend more time with God because we don't see the need.

Think about it this way: Would you agree that spending time with God daily is a good thing to do? Obviously, the answer is yes. Okay. Given that, would you agree that spending time with God daily benefits and blesses your life? Again, the obvious answer is yes. Then would you agree that spending time with God daily is an absolute necessity?

Now, here's where things start to go a little sideways. Once again, we want to say the answer is yes, but do we really believe that? Does the way we live our lives reflect that?

I'm afraid what our lives really communicate is that we believe spending time with God daily is a good *option*. We say to ourselves, *I don't have to spend time with God. I can live today without that. I can make it today on my own.*

There's just one problem with that line of thought—Jesus said the opposite. "Apart from Me you can do nothing" (John 15:5).

I used to read that verse and kind of retranslate it in my head. I would hear it as Jesus saying, "Apart from Me you can't do *big things.*" I would think, *Sure, I need to have Jesus in my life if I really want to accomplish something eternally significant. But today I don't have anything big on the agenda, so today I can make it on my own.*

I've been around Christians long enough to know I'm not the only one who's done some of that retranslating. Of course, when something big does come into our lives—losing a job, receiving a scary diagnosis, having a child in trouble—*then* we have time to spend with Jesus. But during a regular, ordinary, run-of-the mill day or week, spending time with Him is just a good option.

Again, the problem is this: Jesus said that apart from Him, we can do nothing—at all.

Today, my only hope of victory is Christ in me, and that will be my only hope tomorrow. I will fail every day in every area of my life apart from Christ in me. I will fail as a husband, a father, a pastor, a friend, a coworker, a neighbor—anything I try to accomplish on my own. When Jesus lives through me, however, "I can do all things through Him who strengthens me" (Phil. 4:13).

Think about it this way. Do you breathe every day? Of course. If you stop breathing, you stop living. Breathing is so necessary to living that you don't even think about it; you just breathe. Do you eat every day? Of course! Most of us eat multiple times each day. Why do we eat? Because if we stop eating, we stop living. It's a necessity. But then listen to the words of Jesus: "Man shall not live on bread alone, but on every word that proceeds out of the mouth of God" (Matt. 4:4).

Here's the point: today I need God as much as I need food in my body. I need God as much as I need breath in my lungs. I'm desperate for God because I'm nothing without Him. Spending time alone with Him daily is an absolute necessity to experience the abundant life Jesus promised. But too often we don't see the need. We think time with Him is just a good option—if we have the time.

That raises one final question: Why don't we see the need to spend time with God each day?

The answer is pride. Pride says to God, I don't need You. Now, I don't think you start any day by looking up to heaven and saying, "God, I don't need You today. I'm good on my own." But that's in essence what you're saying with your actions—with your life—when you don't spend time with Him.

So I'll ask this question as someone who cares about your spiritual development: Have you spent time alone with God today? If not, read the next sentence out loud: *God, I don't need You today because I'm good on my own.* If you're like me, you probably can't even bring yourself to say those words. But every day that we neglect time in His presence, that's exactly what we say with our lives.

### Christ in the Gospels

One of the key ways we can spend time with God is by reading His Word. And because the Bible is to be the centerpiece of our daily conversation with the Father, I'd like to pass along one practice about reading it Clyde Cranford taught me.

Clyde taught me what he called "pursuing Christ's life in the Gospels." That means pursuing the life of Jesus as recorded in the four Gospels. Just to be clear, he did not teach me to avoid the other parts of Scripture. In my time alone with the Father, I read from the whole Bible. But about every third or fourth book, I go back to a Gospel to glean more truth about the life of Jesus.

Why is that important? Because the Christian life is not me living for Jesus. The Christian life is Jesus living His life in me. I should be constantly seeking to learn more about who He is so the Holy Spirit can conform me to His image.

Let me give you an example of this principle in practice. Currently, I'm reading the Gospel of Matthew in my daily personal time with God. I've read Matthew's Gospel many times, but every time I read it again, the Holy Spirit shows me something new.

You know what I've noticed about Jesus's life in the Gospel this time around? Jesus is never in a hurry. Also, whatever appears to be an interruption in His life becomes part of the Father's plan for Him in that given moment. Jesus had a unique ability to take everything in stride.

As I look at my life, I see the exact opposite. I'm always in a hurry. I feel as though I'm constantly being interrupted. Here's an excerpt from what I wrote in my journal just the other day:

Lord, what am I putting on my agenda today that You did not put there? What am I allowing to dominate my schedule that's not a part of Your plan for me? Because, Lord, You've given me all the time today that I need to accomplish everything You want me to do. If there is something on my schedule today that I cannot get to, it is either something that I put there that You didn't want me to do, or I've let something else get in the way, taking the place of what You really wanted me to do.

That's an example of what I mean when I say pursuing the life of Christ in the Gospels. Beyond showing us the theological significance of the deity, the sinlessness of Jesus, and the historical reality of His death, burial, and resurrection, the Gospels are saturated with the life of Christ—the "in the trenches" story of what Jesus did and why.

The theological significance and the historical reality of the Scriptures are the foundation of our faith, but when reading the Gospels, we sometimes miss the wealth of information about the practical way Jesus lived. The way He talked to people. The way He prayed. The time He spent alone with the Father. How He navigated people with difficult personalities. The humility with which He served others. The thousands of ways Jesus modeled the life He's called us to. Although, as I said before, Jesus is infinitely more than a model, that doesn't diminish the reality that He also modeled what it looks like for a human being to live a life of total dependence on God, allowing the Father to accomplish His work through us for His glory.

## Christ Living through Us

I hope you don't hear me saying you "have to" read your Bible and pray every day to be a good Christian. Just like going to church,

Bible reading and prayer are "get to" things. We get to spend time with God, the Creator of the universe. We get to read His Word, where He's revealed Himself to us. We get to engage Him in conversations through prayer at any moment on any subject.

In other words, these activities are a blessing, not a burden. And the more we abide in Christ each day, the more we'll know Him and deepen our relationship with Him. And the more we know Him and deepen our relationship with Him, the more we'll experience His presence and power working through us to accomplish His will in the world.

Here's an illustration of what I mean when I talk about Jesus living His life through us. My wife and I have four children, and each of them went through a definite stage of independence when they were young. In my house, that stage always seemed to begin with the daily ordeal of tying shoes.

One morning we were scrambling to load up our minivan. I don't remember for sure, but it was likely a Sunday morning, and we were probably trying to get to church. What I do remember, though, is my three-year-old daughter trying to walk out of the house with her shoes untied.

"Come here, sweetheart," I said. "Let me tie your shoes for you."

This was a regular occurrence, but on this particular day my daughter decided to declare a war of independence. "No! I'm going to do it myself!"

Now, I knew she didn't have a clue how to tie her shoelaces, but I also knew that look in her eyes. So I said, "All right, sweetie. Go ahead."

You already know what happened next. She tried—and tried, and tried, and tried. I can still picture her there, her face all scrunched up in concentration. She's squatting and shifting back and forth, trying to get the right angle to make her efforts click. But the shoes were nowhere close to being tied.

Finally, in desperation, she threw the shoes onto the floor and cried, "Daddy! Will you help me?"

I picked her up and held her in my lap. We took each shoe and placed them on her feet. Then, with her little hands in mine, I said, "Here's what you do. You take this end, fold this one over, and pull it through—see how you have to make it tight? Then you make the loop, and then you put your finger right here, and then you pull that loop through. Make sure you pull it tight."

As I let go of her hands, she stayed there in my lap, holding the laces in her fingers a little longer. Then she said, "Daddy, look! I tied my shoe!"

Of course, I had tied that shoe. But in a sense, I did it through her. I said, "Wow, sweetie. Look at that. You tied your shoe."

How many days do we relate to our heavenly Father the same way my daughter related to me as her earthly father? Each day He's waiting to spend time with us, to fill us with His presence and power and manifest Himself through us to accomplish good in this world. He's ready to take our hands in His and provide us with exactly what we need.

Yet too often our attitude is, *No, Daddy. I can do it myself. There's nothing big on the agenda today, so I'll make it on my own.* What happens next? We wind up sitting on the floor in frustration because we failed.

If that's you right now, only one right response will do: crawl back into His presence. Sit in His lap and say, *Daddy, I need You.*

Do you know what will happen if you respond that way and intentionally choose to abide in God's presence rather than strive and push and shove and try to live "for" Him through your own strength? He'll give you grace. James 4:6 says, "God is opposed to the proud, but gives grace to the humble."

Grace is God doing for us, in us, and through us everything we don't have the capacity to do on our own. We just need to let go of our pride, our religion, and our stubborn desire to make our own way. When we do that, God gives grace upon grace.

I know this is true because I've experienced the power of abiding in Christ. But that doesn't mean I don't struggle. Lots of days I wake up with a full calendar, and the last thing I want to do is sit down and be with God. I've learned that when I'm in one of those moments, I need to start my time with God by acknowledging how I'm feeling: *God, I know Your Word teaches me how much I need You. And yet today, everything in my heart is pulling me to walk away from Your Word and go do something else. So, Lord, I choose to sit here, and I ask for Your grace to help me open Your Word. By faith, with humility, I acknowledge that apart from You, I can do nothing today or any other day.*

When we approach God like that, He gives grace. And by that grace, we see the need for time with Him. The more we open His Word and spend time with Him, day after day, the more we get to know Him. And guess what happens next? The more we know Him, the more we love Him. And the more we love Him, the more our lives are conformed to His image.

That's the beauty of abiding in Christ. And that's the goal of the Christian life.

# 4

# Freedom from "Trying"

> We are so activity oriented that we assume we were
> saved for a task we are to perform rather than for a
> relationship to enjoy.
>
> Henry T. Blackaby and Richard Blackaby

I like sports. But growing up in Alabama, I barely knew hockey existed. People skating around on ice just wasn't part of my childhood experience.

But in 2017, Las Vegas's first major professional sports team arrived via the expansion draft of the NHL, and the Vegas Golden Knights were born. This team immediately won the heart of our city, and experiencing the Golden Knights' run to the Stanley Cup Finals during their inaugural season forever endeared my heart to the sport of hockey. I became a passionate fan.

One of my favorite parts of attending a Knights game in person is hearing Carnell Johnson sing the national anthem. His rendition of that great song has earned him the nickname "Golden Pipes"—and trust me, that name is well deserved.

Have you ever been to a live event where the national anthem was sung with power? If so, you know what an experience that can be. Even now, I get chills when I imagine hearing that opening verse, "Oh, say can you see by the dawn's early light . . ." Can you hear it in your mind? Can you remember being caught up as perhaps thousands of people sang those words together?

"The Star-Spangled Banner" was written by Francis Scott Key—although the words were originally written as a poem titled "The Defence of Fort McHenry." The poem commemorated the Battle of Baltimore, an attempt by the British army to capture an important American fort during the War of 1812. When the battle concluded, Key couldn't tell what side had won because of all the smoke, destruction, and death. But then he saw the American flag still flying at the fort, and he knew the Colonial army had prevailed.

What we sing at sporting events, however, is just the first stanza of "The Star-Spangled Banner." It has three additional stanzas, and I think the last one is particularly interesting:

> O thus be it ever when freemen shall stand
> Between their lov'd home and the war's desolation!
> Blest with vict'ry and peace may the heav'n rescued land
> Praise the power that hath made and preserv'd us a nation!
> Then conquer we must, when our cause it is just,
> And this be our motto—"In God is our trust,"
> And the star-spangled banner in triumph shall wave
> O'er the land of the free and the home of the brave.[1]

Can you imagine the reaction in our culture if someone were to sing those words at the start of the Super Bowl? Of course, it's that last line of each stanza that brings home the theme of the song: "O'er the land of the free and the home of the brave."

Freedom is an inspirational concept. It's one of those universal values everyone can embrace and support. Of course, as the veterans in our congregation are right to point out, freedom isn't free. Work and sacrifice are required to both achieve and maintain our freedoms, but those efforts are always worth it.

This book is about choosing to embrace freedom in our lives as followers of Jesus. One of my main goals is to help people let go of the burden of religion and experience true freedom in the Christian life. But freedom from what? What are the specific burdens we can cut away and remove as we pursue a life of abiding, connecting, and sharing?

In this chapter, I'll highlight specific ways religion weighs us down—and the freedom we'll experience when we remove those burdens. I'll focus on the way abiding with Jesus brings us freedom from "trying." Then in chapter 5, I'll focus on freedom from sin and temptation.

## The Burden of Trying

If I had to think of a word that best summarizes America's foundational values, that word would be *freedom*. But if I had to think of a second word, it would be *trying*.

Right now, it seems like everyone is "trying" to do something. Trying to eat better. Trying to lose weight. Trying to stop smoking. Trying to pay off debt. Trying to be more cultured. Trying to be less judgmental or less angry or more spontaneous. Trying to read more. Trying to watch less TV. Trying to get along with a neighbor. Trying to call Mom more often. Trying to save for retirement. Trying to spend more time with the kids.

Trying, trying, trying.

When you think about it, *trying* is a tough word because it implies failure. When people are trying to reach a goal, the goal is important; otherwise it wouldn't be worth trying for. But by definition, it also means those people have not yet reached their goal. They've fallen short. The idea of trying almost carries a sense of desperation.

On the other side of the coin, *trying* can be a reassuring word because it makes us feel like we're at least putting effort into something important. We think, *I may not have lost that weight yet, but I'm trying.* Or *I may not have a great relationship with my son, but I'm trying.* Or *I'm probably going to be working when I'm eighty years old because I have no retirement savings, but at least I'm trying to save.*

Unfortunately, I believe many Christians have incorporated this lifestyle of trying into their relationship with God. They want to live as faithful followers of Jesus—they have the right target in place—but they're trying to reach that target through their own efforts. Even worse, they're aware that they're constantly falling short of the life Jesus promised us in His Word, so they feel the failure of missing the mark even as they push themselves to "keep trying."

I know exactly how such people feel, because I've been one of them. In one period of my life, I was so busy living for Jesus that I had no time to be with Him. I was pastoring my first church, a demanding job that required me to prepare three sermons each week, visit parishioners in hospitals, perform funerals and weddings, counsel, lead a staff, manage a budget, and more. On top of that, I was a young father with three children under the age of five. And if all that wasn't enough, I was also a full-time student commuting to seminary 180 miles four days a week.

On a typical day, I left my house at 6:00 a.m. to drive to school. I spent four or five hours in classes and then made the ninety-mile drive back to arrive at my office in the early afternoon. Until about 6:00 p.m., I dealt with whatever I needed to do in my role as a pastor. Then I went home, spent two hours with my family so I wouldn't feel like a total failure as a husband and father, and then focused on homework until I could no longer stay awake.

Then the next morning, I started the same routine all over again.

I justified all this busyness because I was "doing it for Jesus." But spiritually, I was running on fumes. I was empty inside and had nothing left to give. I felt like I was burning out right when most pastors are getting started.

But it was all okay—because I was "trying."

Have you been in a similar place? Maybe not so busy, but have you spent time trying to read the Bible more? Trying to be more consistent with your prayer life? Trying to have a better attitude about the worship at your church? Trying to stop that addictive behavior that makes you feel so guilty—or at least trying to do it less often? Trying to be more spiritual? Trying to be a better Christian? Trying, trying, trying? If so, you know how heavy the burden of that lifestyle can be. And you know what a blessing it would be to experience freedom from trying.

### Symptoms of Trying

In my experience, people who are trying to live the Christian life almost always feel disillusioned, disappointed, frustrated, and confused because they know they aren't meeting the standards they've set for themselves. Yet they continue to believe they'll get there if they just keep trying.

To make matters worse, many people are encouraged into this lifestyle by pastors, small-group leaders, and spiritual mentors who don't understand what following Jesus is all about—and who themselves are trying to be spiritual. Instead of leading people to the Savior, they push them toward a system of rights and wrongs, dos and don'ts, rules and regulations.

So how do you know if you're caught up in this cycle of trying? In my experience, we need to watch for three main symptoms.

### Symptom 1: Striving to Earn Spiritual Maturity

The first symptom of trying to follow Jesus is believing that spiritual growth and spiritual maturity can be earned. In many ways, people with this approach to following Jesus act as if heaven has a spiritual bank that stores credit in our accounts whenever we do something "spiritual" and deducts from our accounts whenever we sin.

Bill has been a Christian his whole life. His parents were Christians, and he grew up in church. Now in his forties, he considers himself spiritually mature. He's familiar with the Bible, he has no public vices, and he's known as an active member of his church community.

Bill also has an addiction to online pornography. He knows this is both sinful and harmful, and he genuinely would like to have victory over this addiction—but on his terms. For most of the week, he tries his best to resist the temptation. But then his wife takes their children to a movie on Friday night, and Bill indulges while they're away. The next morning, he reads his Bible for an extra thirty minutes. He also confesses his sin during his prayer time and commits to "doing better" the next time he's left alone in the house.

Bill knows he probably won't do better, but that's not the point. The point is that he counts on his extra good behavior to somehow earn back whatever spiritual credit he lost with his bad behavior.

Nancy is up for a promotion at work. She's competing with two of her coworkers for it, and she's done all she can at the office to make her case. During her prayer time, she tells God she'd like to receive the promotion. She even asks Him to provide that blessing if it lines up with His will. Additionally, she spends extra time in prayer throughout the week. She reads her Bible longer and longer each day, and she's careful to avoid anything that could be considered sinful—she even rejects her routine bowl of ice cream each night.

Whether or not she's conscious of it, Nancy is attempting to store up spiritual credit—credit she hopes will allow her to "cash in" and receive the promotion.

In both of these examples, the core misconception is that we can earn spiritual credit with God—either forgiveness or favor—through our own efforts.

### Symptom 2: Experiencing Spiritual Guilt

Constantly feeling guilty is another symptom of trying to be a faithful follower of Jesus. The more we focus on our spiritual scorecards—and on the spiritual scorecards of everyone around us—the more we're aware of falling short.

For Nancy, guilt usually comes when she hears about the high points of other people's spiritual lives. For example, when one of the people in her small group speaks up about sharing the gospel with a coworker, Nancy is genuinely pleased to hear the story. But it also makes her feel guilty and anxious because it's been a long time since she's shared the gospel with one of her coworkers. She feels as if her friend's success has highlighted a weakness in her own spiritual life.

Nancy resolves to have a spiritual conversation with one of her coworkers the next day. She wouldn't phrase it this way, but she feels she's fallen behind her friend in terms of spiritual accomplishments, and she wants to catch up.

Bill often feels guilty when he chooses something he enjoys over the opportunity to do something "spiritual." For example, his favorite football team is playing on *Sunday Night Football*, but his church is having a worship night the same time as the game. Bill decides to stay home and watch the game, but he feels guilty, and he doesn't really enjoy the time to himself.

Bill doesn't know how to articulate this sense of guilt, but he's built his life on a foundation of spiritual performance not only for himself but also for others. Choosing to watch football over attending a church service makes Bill feel guilty and uncomfortable because he perceives it as a missed opportunity to be seen prioritizing spiritual things over his own desires. It makes him feel less mature as a Christian.

### Symptom 3: Developing Spiritual Arrogance

Another common symptom of trying to live the Christian life is developing a level of arrogance when it comes to our spirituality. Whether or not we admit it to ourselves, we start to believe we're ahead of others in terms of being a good Christian—almost as if we view life as a spiritual marathon. We think we're in the top 10 percent of performers. That makes us feel good, and we like that feeling.

Back to Bill. He's been part of a small group with ten or twelve other men for close to a year now. They meet weekly to work through a Bible study, pray for one another, and fellowship. Most of the men are around Bill's age, but he views the group as split into different spiritual levels. In his mind, the group leader is the most spiritually mature, but Bill comes next. He knows several of the other men admire him, and he believes they're right to do so.

Two men in the group are recovering from alcoholism, and another man rarely does any of the assigned homework for the Bible study. Bill sees them at the bottom level of spiritual maturity within the group. When they talk during the study, Bill doesn't give much credence to what they say. Nor does he consider sparking a deeper friendship with any of these three men. Deep down, he believes the differences in their spiritual maturity would prevent them from forming a meaningful connection. Bill is aware that his own troubles with pornography are similar to an alcohol addiction, but he genuinely believes he will "get it under control" in another year or so. He doesn't need to seek outside help.

Nancy regularly interacts with customers and neighbors who aren't Christians. She knows they're not Christians because of how they dress, how they talk, and how they support certain politicians. Deep down, Nancy doesn't like such people. She finds them off-putting and dangerous in a way she doesn't completely understand.

When Nancy interacts with her customers and neighbors, she's kind and polite. She doesn't display her dislike in any public fashion because she believes that would be dishonoring Jesus. She considers herself a good example, and she hopes her actions and attitudes will one day rub off on those who need to become more like her.

## What Jesus Said about Trying

Do you see the danger in these approaches? Do you see how trying to live for Jesus is just another offshoot of religion and spiritual performance as a way of pleasing God? Not surprisingly, Jesus had some devastating words about this method of following Him.

Matthew 7 contains the end of Jesus's Sermon on the Mount—the most famous and best-known sermon of all time. He gathered His followers on the side of a mountain and taught them several foundational principles for life in His kingdom. He included what we know today as the Beatitudes, the command to love our neighbor, and the command to store up treasure in heaven.

Near the end of the sermon, Jesus addressed those who thought they could earn a place in His kingdom through spiritual activity: "Many will say to Me on that day, 'Lord, Lord, did we not prophesy in Your name, and in Your name cast out demons, and in Your name perform many miracles?' And then I will declare to them, 'I never knew you; depart from Me, you who practice lawlessness'" (Matt. 7:22–23).

Look at what the "many" were saying: "Lord, didn't I do all the right things? Didn't I perform all the right spiritual activities? Didn't I read my Bible and go to church and pray and give and everything else I'm supposed to do?" In other words, "Jesus, can't you see that I'm trying?"

Jesus rebuked such an attitude. He said of such people, "I never knew you." Jesus was speaking about a relationship. And that's the crucial lesson we need to learn in a culture that's founded on "trying." Jesus isn't looking at what we do in our spiritual lives; He's asking, *Do I know you? And do you know Me?*

Here's another example of Jesus's thoughts on trying to live the Christian life. Near the beginning of the book of Revelation, Jesus gives the apostle John seven messages to communicate to seven different regional churches of the day. These messages were tailor-made and specific for the culture, strengths, and weaknesses of each church.

Here's what Jesus communicated to the church at Ephesus:

I know your deeds and your toil and perseverance, and that you cannot tolerate evil men, and you put to the test those who call themselves apostles, and they are not, and you found them to be false; and you have perseverance and have endured for My name's sake, and have not grown weary. But I have this against you, that you have left your first love. Therefore remember from where you have fallen, and repent and do the deeds you did at first; or else I am coming to you and will remove your lampstand out of its place—unless you repent. (Rev. 2:2–5)

Now, notice all the "good" things the Ephesian Christians were doing. Look at all the positive actions and activities Jesus highlighted. The Ephesians had "deeds" and "toil" and "perseverance." They worked hard! Not only that, they demonstrated wisdom regarding those they allowed to be leaders in the church—they rooted out false prophets and false teachers instead of being tolerant of every new idea someone had. And perhaps most importantly, the Ephesians kept at it. Even though their lives were based around spiritual activities and striving to do the right thing all the time, they had not "grown weary."

Up to this point in the letter, the Ephesians must have been feeling pretty good. They must have felt gratified that Jesus had noticed everything they were doing—all the ways they were proving themselves to be faithful disciples in His kingdom. I know I'd be at least a little proud if Jesus said those things about me.

Then came verse 4: "But I have this against you, that you have left your first love."

Who was their first love? Jesus Himself, of course. The church is the bride of Christ.

The Christians in Ephesus had spent years perfecting their Christian routines. They probably shopped only at Christian bookstores, listened only to Christian music, and watched only Christian movies. They knew all the right things, and they did all the right things, and they made sure they knew what all the wrong things were so they could avoid doing them.

But in the midst of all that activity, they lost sight of Jesus. They lost the vital connection to Him that sparked their original desire to be faithful followers of Christ. But nobody noticed because they were all so busy trying to live for Him!

The picture painted here would be almost humorous if it weren't so sad.

### The Antidote for Trying

The bad news is that many Christians today would fit in well with the ancient church at Ephesus. They're trying so hard to live the Christian life that they've lost sight of Jesus—and they don't even know it.

The good news is that Jesus gave us the antidote to trying in that same letter to the church at Ephesus. Look again at verse 5: "Therefore remember from where you have fallen, and repent and do the deeds you did at first."

These three specific commands make up Jesus's antidote:

1. **Remember.** Jesus told the Ephesians to "remember from where you have fallen." Do you remember what it was like when you first followed Jesus? You couldn't get enough of Him. He changed your world. But over time, activity replaces intimacy, and we lose that personal experience with our Savior. So Jesus told us to remember where we used to be.

2. **Repent.** Jesus specifically told the Ephesians to "repent." Repentance is a change of mind about our sin that

produces a change of action concerning our sin. When we fall into "trying," we must get honest with God about our poor choices—about substituting doing for being. We must repent of what we are.

3. **Return.** When Jesus said, "Do the deeds you did at first," He wasn't referring to more spiritual activity, to trying harder. The Ephesians had left their first love, meaning Jesus. The solution was to return to abiding in Jesus—to return to that relationship. The "deeds" they did at first were the steps they'd taken when they first accepted Jesus's call to follow Him.

Jesus wanted the Ephesians to remember that they were sinful and needed to repent. They couldn't save themselves at the beginning, and they couldn't earn their way into spiritual maturity now. They needed a Savior. They needed to return to their first love. They needed to return to the good news of the gospel.

The same is true of us when we fall into "trying."

Here's how Paul expressed that good news: "This is good and acceptable in the sight of God our Savior, who desires all men to be saved and to come to the knowledge of the truth" (1 Tim. 2:3–4). Do you see the power here? God desires to have a relationship with you!

But we have the same problem those first disciples had two thousand years ago. The Bible says our sins have separated us from a relationship with God and that we can do nothing in our own strength to fix that. No amount of doing good things and avoiding bad things will earn us enough credit to bridge that gap and reconcile us to God.

Thankfully, that's where the "good news" of the gospel comes in. God loves you, and He wants a relationship with you so much that He did for you what you couldn't do for yourself. In 1 Timothy

2:5–6, Paul went on to say, "There is one God, and one mediator also between God and men, the man Christ Jesus, who gave Himself as a ransom for all, the testimony given at the proper time." A mediator is someone who reconciles broken relationships.

So here's the big picture:

- God created you and desires a relationship with you.
- You're separated from Him because of your sin.
- God loved you so much that He sent Jesus as a mediator.
- Through His death, burial, and resurrection, Jesus dealt with your sin and made the way for you to know God.

Look again at Mark 3:13–14, which we explored in the previous chapter: "He went up on the mountain and summoned those whom He Himself wanted, and they came to Him. And He appointed twelve, so that they would be with Him and that He could send them out to preach." That word *summoned* is loaded with relational significance. In the original Greek, it meant "to call or invite to oneself."

Jesus's call to His first disciples was an invitation "to be with Him." And His invitation to us is the same. It's not an invitation to participate in a religion. It's not an invitation to "get involved in church." It's not an invitation to moral activity or doing the right thing. It's not an invitation to a system of rules and regulations. It's not even an invitation to go to heaven when we die.

The gospel is an invitation to be with Jesus. And that's the antidote for trying to live the Christian life.

Maybe you're saying, *I know all this. I'm already a Christian. What does this have to do with me?* My answer would be this: it's possible to be a Christian and still think the Christian life is based on *trying* to do all the right things. In fact, it happens all the time. Clyde Cranford says it this way: "Unless a new believer is carefully taught and guided after conversion, he will embark upon a journey of self-will and determination to live the Christian life, a journey which will only lead to disillusionment and disappointment."[2]

Do you know God personally? Do you have a relationship with Him? Or are you pursuing a system of dos and don'ts, rights and wrongs, rules and regulations? One of the greatest discoveries you'll ever make is that God didn't invite you into a relationship with Himself because of what you can do for Him; He invited you into a relationship with Himself because He loves you.

If what you're hearing resonates with your soul and you know you have a relationship with Jesus—thank Him. Right now. Thank Him for inviting you into what you could never earn: a personal relationship with Him.

But if you're realizing you don't have a relationship with God, let me give you some instruction. John 1:12 says, "As many as received Him, to them He gave the right to become children of God, even to those who believe in His name." The way into a relationship with God is believing in His name. The way to accept God's invitation is to put your faith in Jesus. This requires you to "repent," as Jesus said in Revelation 2:5. It requires a turning away from your sin and your self-effort and a turning by faith to Jesus. If you've never done that, I encourage you to put down this book and cry out to Jesus. He invites you to accept His invitation right now.

This, too, is the antidote for trying to live a good life in your own strength. You can't do it alone. Christian or not, you need a Savior.

### Unburdened from Trying

Trying our best to live as faithful followers of Jesus doesn't work. It's a burden, a weight that drags us down and produces disappointment and shame.

What, then, happens when we let go of that burden? What happens when we stop trying?

First and foremost, we get to enjoy the full measure of our relationship with Jesus. When we stop throwing so much of our time, energy, and effort into living *for* Jesus, we can savor the joy of being *with* Jesus. We can experience His presence. We can experience His deep and never-ending love for us. And we can experience the wonder of His power flowing through us and accomplishing more with our lives than we could ever dream.

But we receive another benefit when we reject the burden of trying—another blessing. Jesus described that benefit in words that thrill me every time I read them:

> Come to Me, all who are weary and heavy-laden, and I will give you rest. Take My yoke upon you and learn from Me, for I am gentle and humble in heart, and you will find rest for your souls. For My yoke is easy and My burden is light. (Matt. 11:28–30)

When we let go of the burden of "trying," we can experience the blessing of rest.

Don't you love that word? *Rest!* In a world that's constantly pushing and striving and stretching for more, more, more, we get to be the people who rest. And not just rest from work each day, although that certainly is a blessing. We get to have rest for our souls.

That word *yoke* has a double meaning. In Jesus's day, a yoke was a long piece of wood used to connect a team of oxen together. The farmer would place the yoke across the animals' shoulders so he could steer them while they pulled his plow and tilled the soil. But *yoke* was also the word Jewish rabbis used to define their system of beliefs. In that culture, different rabbis taught different ways to obey God and His Word, and each system was called the rabbi's "yoke." Some rabbis were strict about obeying the Torah, so their yoke was heavy. Others weren't as strict, so their yokes were lighter.

Jesus had His own yoke—His own teachings. But the foundation of His yoke is the truth that we can't work our way into God's presence. All we can do is let go of control, admit our limitations, and enter into the presence of our Savior. That's a yoke that's easy and a burden that's light.

Are you weary from trying to live the Christian life? Are you heavy-laden from rules and systems and religious traditions? Let it all go. Choose to abide in Jesus, and He will give you rest.

# 5

# Freedom from Sin and Temptation

It is not possible for anyone to have such a transaction with Christ as to enable him to say, either, "I am without sin," or, "I can never sin again." This miracle is sustained and continued in our life only by our continuing, moment-by-moment faith in our Savior for his moment-by-moment victory over the power of our sin.

Charles Trumbull

I've noticed that people living in other areas of the country often have one or two misconceptions about the city I call home—Las Vegas. Actually, they can have a whole bucketful of misconceptions.

For example, some visitors are surprised by the terrain. They thought Las Vegas was an oasis way out in the middle of a desert wasteland with nothing but flat sand extending as far as the eye can see. But Las Vegas is surrounded by mountains, canyons, and other interesting landscapes. Because of those formations, the sunsets in Las Vegas are some of the most beautiful on earth.

Another common misconception is that the city is filled entirely with casinos, wedding chapels, and buffet restaurants. Many people have seen pictures or videos of "the Strip," and they're often under the impression that the whole city looks like that. But Las Vegas has a lot in common with most larger cities in the United States—large and small businesses spread out all over the metropolitan area, and we have plenty of housing, schools, parks, malls, and hospitals.

In many ways, Las Vegas is just a normal city—but with a distinct downtown.

Of course, I need to address one more major misconception about Las Vegas, having to do with the main subject of this chapter: sin.

### Two Types of Burdens

The biggest misconception about Las Vegas also happens to be the city's unofficial tagline: "What happens in Vegas stays in Vegas." Unfortunately, this is the lie many people choose to swallow when they come to "Sin City."

Let me make this clear: in no place on earth are sinful choices magically separated from the consequences of those choices. This might be especially true in Las Vegas. Through both stories of people who've visited our city and stories of people who live here, I've seen the truth too many times to have any doubts about that.

The reality is that sin creates a burden in our lives—especially when our sin gives birth to sinful patterns, habits, and strongholds. I've seen people weighed down by financial crisis because they bought into the seductive lie of materialism or because what started as a harmless good time quickly blossomed into a desperate situation. I've seen men and women weighed down by terror at the thought of their spouses learning about the choices they made the night before. And I've seen people of all ages weighed down by the grinding, never-ending pull of drug and alcohol addiction.

Each of those is a heavy burden, and each is rooted in what the Bible calls sin.

But we can carry another, more subtle type of burden related to sin, and it can be just as destructive as those sinful choices that come to mind when you wonder about Las Vegas and what people do here.

That second type of burden occurs when Christians believe the most important part of following Jesus is *not sinning*. As we saw in the previous chapter, our primary goal as followers of Jesus should be to get to know Him. But many Christians incorrectly assume that the goal of the Christian life is to *not* sin. These individuals focus all their energy, effort, and willpower into their personal battle against sin each day—and they often encourage others to make not sinning the main priority in their lives as well.

You've heard enough from me by now to know that a life spent working toward the goal of avoiding sin is just another form of religion. It's another way of living *for* Jesus rather than allowing Jesus to live *through* us. It's another way of making the Christian life all about conformity to a system of rules and regulations.

In other words, basing our lives around not sinning is another heavy burden.

Thankfully, we can experience freedom from both of these burdens rooted in sin when we choose to abide in Christ rather than settle for our own strength.

**Tough Questions**

I mentioned earlier that I met with Clyde Cranford every Thursday afternoon for more than two years. On most of those afternoons, Clyde walked into my office looking somewhat disheveled and unkempt. I often thought of him as an absentminded professor. But there was nothing absent about Clyde's mind once he started teaching.

One particular afternoon, Clyde asked me a series of questions that made me feel as though I was in one of those dark, damp interrogation rooms with only a spotlight shining on my face—and that was just after the first question! The intensity ratcheted up with each question.

### *Does a Christian Want to Sin?*

The first question Clyde asked me was, "Vance, do you want to sin?"

I didn't know what to say. Part of me wanted to shout "No!" because I wanted Clyde to think of me as way too spiritual to want to sin. But then I thought, *I must want to sin, right? Otherwise temptation wouldn't be tempting.* So, wanting to sound theologically correct, I blurted, "Well, of course I want to sin. If I didn't want to sin, it wouldn't be tempting."

Clyde just nodded for a moment. Then he explained that my answer was only partially true. He pointed out that part of me still held a longing for sin, what theologians often refer to as "the flesh." But he also said that, as a Jesus follower, I was much more than just my flesh because the Spirit of Christ lived in me. God Himself was changing me from the inside out.

"Because Christ now lives in us," Clyde told me, his voice as calm and soft as always, "we long for what He longs for. And the things Jesus longs for are not sinful." Clyde explained that one of the things Jesus was changing about me was what I desired—what I wanted. With Christ in me, I now longed for what He longed for. And He never longs for sin.

I realized Clyde was right. Even more, I realized I had proof that he was right. Whenever I did choose to sin as a Jesus follower, I almost immediately felt unhappy with that sin. In other words, my flesh *thought* I wanted to sin, but the minute I went through with it, I realized that sin wasn't really what I wanted.

"So," Clyde asked me again, "does a Christian want to sin?" And this time I knew the answer: "No."

### Does a Christian Have to Sin?

Then Clyde asked, "Vance, do you have to sin?"

Having failed in my first attempt to answer Clyde's initial question, I hesitated on this one. Clyde sensed my hesitation, and he gave me a little help. He asked me to look up these Scriptures to help clarify my response:

- "Knowing this, that our old self was crucified with Him, in order that our body of sin might be done away with, so that we would no longer be slaves to sin; for he who has died is freed from sin" (Rom. 6:6–7).

- "No temptation has overtaken you but such as is common to man; and God is faithful, who will not allow you to be tempted beyond what you are able, but with the temptation will provide the way of escape also, so that you will be able to endure it" (1 Cor. 10:13).

As I read God's Word, two phrases jumped off the page and flashed in front of my eyes: "he who has died is freed from sin" and "with the temptation will provide the way of escape also, so that you will be able to endure it." I knew what Clyde wanted me to see, but I had a hard time accepting what I'd read.

A stirring in my heart made me want to cry out, "No! I don't have to sin!" I'd just read that God was faithful to provide a way of escape at every moment of temptation and weakness in my life. This meant my ability to overcome sin wasn't rooted in my faithfulness to God but in God's faithfulness to me. In Christ, every time I was tempted to sin, I had the freedom to experience victory over sin.

But the seminary degree hanging on the wall of my office had taught me a theological term I couldn't reconcile with what I'd just read: *depravity*. *Depravity* means that apart from the grace of God, every person on this earth would run headlong into every form of wickedness. I believed that was true then, and I believe it's true now. Apart from God's grace in my life, I will always choose to sin.

I asked myself again, *Do I have to sin?* Depravity means I will always choose to sin apart from God's grace, but I wasn't—nor am I now—apart from God's grace!

My understanding of depravity had convinced me sinning was a guaranteed part of the human experience—something I should accept as normal. But as I continued to wrestle with these ideas in my heart, it was as if the Holy Spirit turned on a light inside me. I remembered Romans 5:2, which says it's this grace "in which we stand."

As a Jesus follower, I never have to live apart from the grace of God. I've been rooted and planted in the amazing grace of God, and I will never live another second apart from it.

Clyde must have seen that I was beginning to understand, because he quoted 2 Peter 1:2–3: "Grace and peace be multiplied to you in the knowledge of God and of Jesus our Lord; *seeing that*

*His divine power has granted to us everything pertaining to life and godliness*, through the true knowledge of Him who called us by His own glory and excellence" (emphasis added).

I felt the stirring in my heart again. According to Peter, the moment I came to know Jesus as Savior, He gave me everything I could ever need pertaining to life and godliness. In other words, the moment I came to know Him, Jesus gave me everything I would ever need to live a godly life through the presence of His Holy Spirit inside me.

Does a Christian have to sin? I looked at Clyde and said, "No."

## Why Do We Sin?

Clyde had hit me right between the eyes with his questions twice, and now he zeroed in on me again with a third question that stopped me in my tracks. "Vance, if you don't want to sin and you don't have to sin, why do you sin?"

I had no answer.

## Love and Obey

I remember feeling like hours had passed in silence as I sat in that room with Clyde. It was probably less than a minute, but my world had been rocked. I was stunned.

*If I don't want to sin and I don't have to sin, then why do I sin?*

Eventually, Clyde opened my Bible and pointed to John 14:15. He asked me to read this verse out loud: "If you love Me, you will keep My commandments."

Now, I was already familiar with that verse. But until that moment, I had always heard Jesus saying, *If you love Me, you better obey Me!* I had always placed the emphasis on obedience. If I truly loved Jesus, I would prove that love by obeying His commandments.

Now I realize this idea is at the core of every major religion in the world. You must show God you love Him by obeying Him, and then you earn His acceptance. If you love God, you better _____. Religion fills in the blank with dos and don'ts, rights and wrongs, rules and regulations. But that's the way I had always understood that verse. As a result, the focus of my life as a follower of Jesus had always been on trying hard to obey Him. I felt a burden to show God how much I loved Him by trying to do all the right things and not do all the wrong things. And the more I tried, the more I failed. That didn't work.

This time, when I read that verse out loud, I heard the tender voice of Jesus—that still, small voice whispering into my soul— saying, *If you simply love Me, obedience will spill from your life.* This time, I heard the emphasis on *loving Jesus*, not on *obeying Him*. When you understand what He said that way, obedience is no longer the focus of your life as a follower of Jesus. Obedience becomes the fruit of your life once you focus on intimacy with Him. This in no way suggests that obedience is unimportant in the life of a believer. It just reveals that obedience isn't the focus of your life as a believer. Loving Jesus is the focus.

I've never forgotten the next words Clyde spoke, and I never will. He said, "Our obedience is in direct proportion to our love." This means if I'm struggling in an area of obedience, I don't have an obedience problem; I have a love for Jesus problem. In other words, I love my sin more than I love Him.

Clyde made it clear that the reason I sinned was because I didn't love God. And when he said that, I got angry—enough to think about leaping across my desk, getting in his face, and shouting, "How dare you say that! Don't you realize how hard I've tried to live the Christian life? Don't you understand the work I've put into trying to obey Him?"

But I quickly realized my problem wasn't Clyde. It wasn't even that he had pointed out this truth in my life. My problem was that the words convicting me to my core came straight from the lips of Jesus: "If you love Me, you will keep My commandments."

That moment was a gracious invitation from Jesus to go deeper in my love relationship with Him than I had ever been before. And I'm so grateful and so blessed that He gave me that opportunity—and that I said yes.

### The Merry-Go-Round of the Flesh

Here's the truth I learned from Clyde that day: I don't have to sin, and I don't have to live a life dedicated to the pursuit of not sinning. What freedom to have those burdens removed!

But as Jesus followers, we have to account for another truth: we're engaged in a battle every day. Yes, we receive grace from our Savior, and through Him we're free from the power of sin. That's true. But at the same time, we still possess a sinful nature on this side of eternity. Again, this is what theologians refer to as "the flesh," and our flesh has declared war against our Savior. The sinful part of us longs to separate us from Christ and His grace, so we're in a battle every moment of every day, where we have to deal with the temptation to go back to our old way of life and live apart from Christ in us.

How do we fight that battle? Not by "trying." This is not religion. The key to victory begins with our time alone with Jesus. We fight not by trying but by trusting that the key to victory is abiding in Christ.

And if we're serious about abiding in Christ, we need to break free from what I call the Merry-Go-Round of the Flesh.

Here's what typically happens when we're constantly tempted to skip spending time with God. We read a book about following Jesus—maybe even a book like the one you're holding. Or we go to a conference on spiritual growth or listen to a sermon about spending time with God. Then we think, *That is so right. That's exactly what I needed to hear. That is so where I'm living right now. Starting tomorrow morning, I'll always carve out time. I'll get my Bible and my notebook, and I'll be ready. I'm going to spend time with God.*

For a few days, we do pretty well. We even walk into church thinking, *Man, I spent time with God seven days this week. I did it! I'm doing great.*

Then what happens? We fail. We blow it. We miss a day. Maybe two. Then we become discouraged and think, *Man, I could've done so much better. Why am I such a bad Christian? Why can't I live like everybody else? Why do I always fail?*

This whole routine is a cycle of spiritual ups and downs—and it's vicious. We repeat it over and over. We "try" and then get discouraged. Then once again, somehow, we hear about spending time with the Father. We think, *That's so true. Why didn't I get it last time? I'm going to do it now. I'll find an accountability partner to hold me accountable to spending time with God every day.*

During this next cycle, we may make it two weeks, three weeks, even a month. It's going so well that we might even go to our pastor and say, "I think I need to lead a group on how to spend time with God, because I'm so consistent now! I haven't missed a day. My system is working."

Then what happens? We fail again. We go back to those dark places of discouragement, despondency, and spiritual depression. *Seriously, why can't I do better?* And the cycle repeats. And repeats. And repeats—over and over again.

Does this sound familiar? Do you feel trapped on this spiritual roller coaster? Do you hear all the "I"s in the cycle above? *I should do better. I'm going to do it. I'm doing great.*

Let me show you this Merry-Go-Round of the Flesh:

## Merry-Go-Round of the Flesh

Do you know what keeps us on this merry-go-round? Pride. The belief that we can fix our problems by ourselves, that we don't need help. We'll get it if we just keep trying.

If you resonate at all with this concept, with this cycle, don't be discouraged. There's another way.

Let's try this again. Tomorrow morning, like me, you might wake up with the temptation to skip spending time with God. But this time you won't muster your willpower and say, *I'm going to do it!* This time you'll humbly say, *Lord, I can't do it. In my own strength, I won't do it. I know me. I'll fail. Apart from You, God, I can do nothing. But through You, I can do all things.*

When you approach God with this sense of humility, remember what He promises to do. He gives grace. And when He gives grace, you experience victory. Victory! And when you experience victory over temptation in that area of your life and others see the transformation, they'll say, "Man, something is changing in you! What's happening?" Your response will no longer be, "Well, I've got a good system for how to have quiet time." No, your response will be, "It's not me; it's Christ in me." And then God gets all the glory.

Here's a principle we all need to remember: a life of humility before Christ always leads to a life of victory in Christ. This doesn't mean we'll no longer be tempted. It doesn't mean we'll no longer have to battle against our sinful nature. Victory doesn't mean deliverance. But it does mean we now have a new way to win the battle, moment by moment. It's not us; it's Christ in us.

This is what my mentor called the Ascending Spiral of Grace:

### Ascending Spiral of Grace

The Ascending Spiral of Grace can be experienced only as you live moment by moment. You'll find it when you declare, *Lord, I can't. I won't. But I know You can, so I'm trusting You will.*

Please hear this: it's time for you to stop trying to live the Christian life. Instead, surrender yourself to Christ so He can live His life through you. In every moment of temptation, stop trying in your own strength and start trusting in His power. Let me tell you what you'll find if you do that—rest. A yoke that's easy. A burden that's light. That's the freedom available to you in Christ. It's yours!

As someone who spent years riding my own Merry-Go-Round of the Flesh and experiencing all the discouragement and frustration that came with it, let me say that there's no joy like the joy of abiding in Christ on the Ascending Spiral of Grace.

Welcome to the ride of your life!

## Intimacy with God

As we conclude this section on our key word *Abide*, look once again at John 14:15: "If you love Me, you will keep My commandments." Jesus repeated that truth over and over in this chapter. For example, here's what He said in verse 21: "He who has My commandments and keeps them is the one who loves Me; and He who loves Me will be loved by My Father, and I will love him and will disclose Myself to him."

In that verse, Jesus made a promise to "disclose" Himself. The word *disclose* means to make known. So the more I pursue Christ, the more He makes Himself known to me. And the more Christ makes Himself known to me, the more I love Him. And the more I love Him, the more obedience spills out of my life because of His grace.

Do you see how this just makes sense? This is exactly how Jesus intended for us to grow as His followers. Not by obeying first, but by first seeking Him and allowing Him to produce obedience through us.

Then Jesus added another layer in verse 23: "Jesus answered and said to him, 'If anyone loves Me, he will keep My word; and My Father will love him, and We will come to him and make Our abode with him.'"

Here we have this progression again. When we love God and pursue Him, He not only produces obedience through us but blesses us with His presence. He makes His "abode" with us—His home. This verse is describing someone saturated with God's presence.

Another way to describe this is intimacy with God. Have you ever been around someone and just sensed the presence of God all over them? That's the level of relationship Jesus was describing in these verses. It's not that those people participate in more spiritual activity or have more biblical knowledge; those aren't key. Those who experience intimacy with God consistently practice being with Jesus. And God promises that, when He finds someone who consistently practices being with Christ, He'll manifest His presence all over their life.

The outcome of abiding in Christ is experiencing intimacy with God. And that's the ultimate rejection of religion.

Now look at the final verse of John 14, verse 31. Jesus said, "So that the world may know that I love the Father, I do exactly as the Father commanded Me." At the end of this teaching, Jesus drove home this relationship between love and obedience by using His own life as an example. This pattern of living is exemplified in Jesus. He pursued a loving relationship with God the Father during His public ministry on earth, which resulted in a life of obedience to the Father's will. That was Jesus's life. And guess what He's invited us to experience? A love relationship with God that results in a life of obedience to His will.

In other words, Jesus invited us into the exact same life He lived—and still lives. The life of a Jesus follower is the life of Jesus.

What we've made so complicated, Jesus boiled down to this one foundational relationship between Him and the Father—and now between us, as His followers, and the Father. The key to that relationship is for us to intentionally, actively, and consistently abide in Him.

# PART 3

# CONNECT

Therefore, brethren, since we have confidence to enter the holy place by the blood of Jesus, by a new and living way which He inaugurated for us through the veil, that is, His flesh, and since we have a great priest over the house of God, let us draw near with a sincere heart in full assurance of faith, having our hearts sprinkled clean from an evil conscience and our bodies washed with pure water. Let us hold fast the confession of our hope without wavering, for He who promised is faithful; and let us consider how to stimulate one another to love and good deeds, not forsaking our own assembling together, as is the habit of some, but encouraging one another; and all the more as you see the day drawing near.

Hebrews 10:19–25

# 6

## You Belong to God's Family

> The Word, the gospel, creates not just *people* individually, but *a people*, collectively.
>
> Matt Chandler

My wife, Kristie, and I have four children: Hannah, Caleb, Elijah, and Faith. Each of them is unique in their own way. We have everything from introverts to athletes, musicians to gamers, and Crossfitters to foodies. But one common factor, other than Jesus, unites us in a strong and unbreakable bond: a deeply rooted passion for Alabama football.

Every Saturday afternoon in the fall, a gathering—filled with rituals, traditions, and festivities of all kinds—takes place in our living room. Over the years, we've been privileged to invite our children's friends to attend these gatherings and sometimes other visitors as well, but our family sits at the foundation.

I don't want to give away any secrets, but we have a kickoff ritual and many touchdown rituals. We also have halftime festivities, and, of course, game-winning celebrations. One of our most important rituals, though, involves a Houndstooth hat and a pair of Alabama wide-receiver gloves. The hat and gloves are reserved only for certain situations. You might say they're set apart. If there's ever a time of desperation in the game—like victory is on the line and Alabama needs to make a play—that's when we bring out the hat and gloves. And no, we're not superstitious; we're just cautious.

One of the joys of my life has been the fact that, as our family continues to grow, this deep-seated passion for Alabama football is passed on. My son-in-law, born and raised in the western United States, is now a passionate fan of the Crimson Tide. My daughter-in-law, whose family is from the Philippines, likewise is a devoted fan. And perhaps my greatest joy is that my beautiful granddaughter, Karis Grace, is being taught to say "Roll Tide." I look forward to even more generations of devoted fans.

My family is a gift, and the time I'm privileged to spend in their presence is an incredible blessing in my life. In a similar way, Jesus followers can enjoy the amazing blessing of being included in God's family—the church.

Remember, the key word for this concept is *Connect*. And as we'll see over the next few chapters, one of the incredible blessings we receive as Jesus followers is the privilege of having a relationship not only with God but also with members of His family.

## Not Alone

Several years ago, John Eldredge published a short book titled *Epic*. Its premise is that you and I are part of a much bigger story than our own—God's story. And in thinking about God's family, I like what Eldredge writes about God and this idea of it not being good for us to be alone:

> Now, I have a confession to make. Ever since I began to believe in God . . . I have pictured God as . . . alone. Sovereign, powerful, all that. But by himself. Perhaps the notion sprang from the fact that I felt myself to be alone in the universe. Or perhaps it came from the religious images of God seated on a great throne way up there . . . somewhere. How wonderful to discover that God has never been alone. He has always been Trinity—Father, Son, and Holy Spirit. God has always been a fellowship. The whole Story began with something *relational*.[1]

When Eldredge writes, "The whole Story began with something *relational*," he was referring to Genesis 1, where Scripture first reveals that God is not only a Person but a Community of Persons: "Then God said, 'Let Us make man in Our image'" (v. 26). *Let Us. Our image.* In the very first chapter of God's Word to us, He revealed Himself to be a relational Being.

This aspect of God's nature is what theologians call the Trinity. It means God exists as three distinct Persons in one unique Being—the Father, the Son, and the Holy Spirit. This reality can sometimes be difficult to understand, and that's okay. It makes sense that God is mysterious and beyond our comprehension.

But the Bible is clear about this aspect of God's nature—He is one Being who exists in three Persons. For example, Deuteronomy 6:4 shows us that God is one Being: "Hear, O Israel! The LORD is our God, the LORD is one!" Similarly, Galatians 3:20 says, "Now a mediator is not for one party only; whereas God is only one." Clearly, God is one Being.

At the same time, and as we've already seen in Genesis 1, God speaks about Himself as "Us" many times in the Bible. Not only that, but many times all three Persons of the Trinity are mentioned together. For example, Isaiah 61:1 is the beginning of a prophecy pointing forward to Jesus, the Messiah. It says, "The Spirit of the Lord God is upon me, because the Lord has anointed me to bring good news to the afflicted; He has sent me to bind up the brokenhearted, to proclaim liberty to captives and freedom to prisoners."

Probably the best example of an interaction between the Persons of the Trinity is found at Jesus's baptism before the start of His public ministry:

> After being baptized, Jesus came up immediately from the water; and behold, the heavens were opened, and he saw the Spirit of God descending as a dove and lighting on Him, and behold, a voice out of the heavens said, "This is My beloved Son, in whom I am well-pleased." (Matt. 3:16–17)

Why is it important for us to accept the reality of the Trinity? Because God is a relational Being, and He created us in His image—in His likeness. That means we were created for relationships, hard-wired to live in community. Scripture makes that clear in the next chapter of Genesis: "Then the Lord God said, 'It is not good for the man to be alone'" (2:18).

That Hebrew word translated "good" can also be translated "best." So let me ask you this: Would you like to experience the absolute best life possible? I don't think anyone would say, "Nah. I'll settle for average. I'll take a C+ life." We all want the best life possible. With that in mind, understand that at the beginning of beginnings, here's what God said about us: apart from fellowship and relationships with others, we will never know the best life He has for us. He said it's not good, it's not best, for man to be alone. The word *alone* means to be separated from others, without the help and support of other people.

The bottom line is that the best God has for you will never be experienced apart from relationships with others. Think about it. Even people who don't follow Jesus say the real meaning of life is found in relationships with other people—connection with family, with friends, with people they care about.

Without relationships, life has little meaning, significance, or value. That's true for all of humanity, and the truth only intensifies as we're conformed to the image of Christ through our relationship with God.

This is yet another reason I keep saying the life of a Jesus follower is all about relationships.

### The Birth of the Church

This idea that it's not good for human beings to be without other human beings goes beyond the book of Genesis. It's a theme we find over and over throughout the Scriptures.

Let's focus on the events described in Acts 2, which many consider to be the birth of the New Testament church. These events took place in Jerusalem on what's called the day of Pentecost. The chapter begins with a major moment, when God's Holy Spirit is poured out on the disciples in a powerful and supernatural way. They were supercharged with God's Spirit, and they burst onto the streets of Jerusalem speaking and shouting about the glorious things God had done. Much of the chapter is recorded as a poignant sermon from the apostle Peter in which he calls his Jewish brethren to recognize that Jesus is the Messiah, God's chosen Savior, and begs them to repent of their sins of rejecting Him and murdering Him on the cross.

Many in Jerusalem responded to Peter's message: "So then, those who had received his word were baptized; and that day there were added about three thousand souls" (Acts 2:41). These people embraced the truth of the gospel. They received Jesus as Lord and Savior. They were born again into a relationship with God. And then the Bible says they were "added."

Now, it's important for us to understand that when the Greek word translated "added" is used here, it's in the passive voice. That means the subject is *receiving* the action rather than *doing* the action. So when the Bible records that these people were "added," it means they didn't add themselves *to* something; they were added *by* Someone. The moment they began following Jesus, God supernaturally, by His Spirit, added them to something.

The word *add* can also be translated "to join together with." The Bible uses the same term again in Acts 2:47: "And the Lord was adding to their number day by day those who were being saved." We need to ask what they were being added to. With whom was God joining them together? The answer is that they were added to the community of believers—to the church. Within the context of the city of Jerusalem, a new family had been created: the family of God. And every time someone began a relationship with God, He immediately added that person to His family in a supernatural way.

The same is true today. When someone becomes a Christian in your church or community, God instantly adds that person to His family.

We use the term *born again* to describe the way salvation frees us from the bondage of sin and makes us new as followers of Jesus. I like that term because it's so relational. When babies are born, they don't enter this world in isolation. They're born into a family. They have a mom and a dad, grandparents, siblings, cousins, aunts and uncles. In the same way, Christians are born into God's family.

Here's an important point: the New Testament knows nothing of Christianity without community. Nothing. It's not an option. Being a Christian is entirely relational, beginning with our relationship with Jesus and then including our relationships within the church.

The New Testament is saturated with biblical community. It opens with four Gospels detailing the life, death, burial, and resurrection of Jesus—all of which brings us into a right relationship with God. Then the book of Acts introduces us to the beginning of New Testament community in Jerusalem—the church. Finally, every other book in the New Testament was written either to address a community of believers or to bring about change within the context of a community of believers.

Consider the book of Galatians. It's a letter written to the community of believers in Galatia. The book of Romans is a letter written to the community of believers in Rome. The books of 1 and 2 Thessalonians are letters written to the community of believers in Thessalonica.

Maybe you're now thinking I forgot about letters to individuals, such as the two epistles Paul wrote to Timothy: *they weren't written to communities!* No, I didn't forget those letters. They were written to establish leadership in the community of believers and to describe both how that leadership was to lead and how the body of Christ was to function. They were intended to support and to bring about change within the church.

Now maybe you're thinking, *You forgot about the book of Philemon! It was written to one guy.* You are correct. But do you know what that letter is about? Philemon and another brother named Onesimus had experienced brokenness in their relationship. Paul was writing to Philemon, challenging him to pursue reconciliation with his brother in Christ. The book is entirely relational.

Every New Testament letter is written either about or to affect a community of believers. And let me say it again: God created us to enjoy our relationship with Him in the context of our relationships with our brothers and sisters in Christ.

**Reality #1:** *Because I have a relationship with God, I now have a relationship with God's family.*

As we work through the Connect portion of our journey toward faithfully following Jesus, we'll focus on some important realities that exist in the life of a believer because of God's emphasis on community. And please pay attention to that word *realities*. These are not possibilities. They're truths grounded in Scripture.

Here's the first reality: *Because I have a relationship with God, I now have a relationship with God's family.*

If you're a follower of Jesus, you belong to the family of God. In John 1:12, the apostle John writes this about those who receive Jesus: "As many as received Him, to them He gave the right . . ." Before we read further, pay attention to the word *right*. It means power, authority, or liberty. It's a judicial term. Here's John again: "As many as received Him, to them He gave the right to become children of God, even to those who believe in His name."

So the Bible says the moment I began a relationship with God through Jesus Christ, God gave me the right—the legal standing—to be called His child.

One of the great joys of my life is that God in His grace invited my family to join in His activity of planting and pastoring Hope Church here in Las Vegas. And one of the blessings of being part of Hope Church is that we've started more than sixty churches out of our congregation. We are a church-planting church.

Zeke Tomaselli came to Christ at Hope Church, he was discipled at Hope Church, and he met his wife, Layne, and married her at Hope Church. But Zeke is originally from Hilo, Hawaii, and God burdened his and Layne's hearts for his hometown. As a result, a couple of years ago Hope Church sent Zeke and Layne to Hilo to help plant Ohana Church. I'm pleased to say that God is blessing this new fellowship. And guess what? Now they're planting new churches out of *their* church. They're working within the Pacific Rim to reach people who have never heard the gospel.

One of the ways God continued to bless Zeke and Layne was by leading them to serve their community through the foster care system. Zeke and Layne fostered three little boys for some time, and eventually God led them to pursue adoption. After a long process, they stood before a judge who declared those boys officially part of the Tomaselli family—or as they like to say, their "ohana." Those three little boys now have the right to be called the sons of Zeke and Layne. That means everything Zeke and Layne have belongs to them as well. A judicial act took place. They were outside that family, but now they've been brought into that family. They are Tomasellis.

In the same way, the moment you were born again in a relationship with God—the moment you turned away from your sin—God made a declarative judgment to adopt you into His family. You are now called a son or daughter of God. And get this, everything that belongs to Him now belongs to you! Because you have a relationship with God, you now have a relationship with God's family.

Please don't hear me say this reality diminishes our connections within our birth families or the families that adopted us. That's not the case. I'm simply stating that we, as followers of Jesus, are part of a bigger family. When we read the Bible's stories about Moses, Abraham, David, Jonah, Jesus, Peter, and Paul, we're reading the history of our family. When we travel overseas and meet brothers and sisters in Christ, we're visiting our family. When we read in the book of Revelation that we're going to gather around the throne of God with King Jesus and reign with Him one day, we're reading the future of our family. Why? Because that's who we are. We belong to the family of God.

Romans 8:15 says, "You have not received a spirit of slavery leading to fear again." Unfortunately, that's exactly where many Christians live—in slavery and fear. They think, *Now I've got this relationship with God. Now He's the boss and I'm just supposed to do everything He says. I must focus on being obedient.* Listen, I'm not saying obedience isn't important, but that's not the main thing. That's not the spirit we've been given. You don't have to live in fear of God.

Look what Paul said in the rest of Romans 8:15: "You have received a spirit of adoption as sons by which we cry out, 'Abba! Father!'" Now, *Abba* is a Greek word that means Papa or Daddy. It's a term of intimacy and endearment. So based on this verse in God's Word, when we become a follower of Jesus, we can approach God and say, "Daddy!" We have the legal right to approach Him that way. Look at what Paul says next in verse 16: "The Spirit Himself testifies with our spirit that we are children of God."

Here's the point: following Jesus means you belong to the family of God. Say that out loud: "I belong to the family of God." Say it one more time: "I belong to the family of God."

This is such good news! Right now, today, you don't have any responsibility to work your way into the family of God. You're in! Your status in God's family isn't rooted in your performance; it's rooted in your position in Christ. You and I legally belong to the family of God.

### The Blessing of "One Another"

In 1939, Harvard University commissioned a research project that became the longest study of adult human development in the history of research. This project continued for 75 years, studying the development of 724 men—456 from Boston's poorest neighborhoods and 268 Harvard graduates. Interestingly, the project continued for so long that it outlived the researchers who began it!

In 2014, this incredible research project finally came to an end. In a recent TED Talk, Robert Waldinger, the current director of the Harvard Study of Adult Development, shared some of the results from that study:

> What are the lessons that come from the tens of thousands of pages of information that we've generated on these lives? Well, the lessons aren't about wealth or fame or working harder and harder. The clearest message that we get from this 75-year study is this: good relationships keep us happier and healthier. Period. . . . Relationships are messy and they're complicated. . . . But over and over, over these 75 years, our study has shown that the people who fared the best were the people who leaned in to relationships, with family, with friends, with community. . . . The good life is built with good relationships.[2]

I find it fascinating that it took Harvard University 75 years of research and millions of dollars to conclude the same central truth we've been exploring from God's Word—the life of a Jesus follower is all about relationships.

But we need to address another question before we conclude this chapter: What benefits do we receive from our relationships within the church? Harvard's research found that the good life is built through good relationships. The Bible, an infinitely higher authority than Harvard University, reveals that we'll never experience the best life God has for us apart from relationships with our brothers and sisters in Christ. But what makes these relationships so significant?

> Those who had received his word were baptized; and that day there were added about three thousand souls. They were continually devoting themselves to the apostles' teaching and to fellowship, to the breaking of bread and to prayer.
>
> Everyone kept feeling a sense of awe; and many wonders and signs were taking place through the apostles. And all those who had believed were together and had all things in common; and they began selling their property and possessions and were sharing them with all, as anyone might have need. Day by day continuing with one mind in the temple, and breaking bread from house to house, they were taking their meals together with gladness and sincerity of heart, praising God and having favor with all the people. And the Lord was adding to their number day by day those who were being saved. (Acts 2:41–47)

Before we go any further, notice that community is not what we *do* as a church; community is who we *are*. When the first believers came together in Jerusalem, community just happened. As these people began a relationship with God, that connection spilled out of their lives into fellowship relationships with their new brothers and sisters in Christ. They didn't have a fancy program. They didn't have a perfect structure. This was the church being the church, living life in community.

Next, look at what the members of that earliest church experienced together. They devoted themselves to four important priorities: the apostles' teaching, fellowship, breaking bread, and prayer.

First, they benefited by exploring God's Word and helping one another learn the truth of the gospel. They grew together spiritually.

Then they spent time together. And they didn't always do "serious" and "churchy" things, either; they took time just to be together. They enjoyed one another's company.

Next, they broke bread together—and that phrase means exactly what you think it means. They ate! They had church potlucks! They used meals to both connect with one another and minister together.

And finally, they prayed together. Yes, prayer can be a personal conversation between us and God. But prayer can also be—and should be on a regular basis—joining together corporately before God and talking with Him together.

Now, doesn't that sound like a community worth experiencing? Teaching, fellowship, eating, and prayer. All those together create an incredible foundation for our relationships with one another as members of God's family.

I just used a phrase I've used many times throughout this chapter: "one another." And that's intentional, because the New Testament is filled with "one another" passages that help us understand the benefits of living together in relationship as members of God's family. These passages were written by Mark, John, Paul, Peter, and James, to name a few, and they help us see what life in community is supposed to look like.

Here are just a few of those passages:

- "This is My commandment, that you love one another, just as I have loved you" (John 15:12).
- "As each one has received a special gift, employ it in serving one another as good stewards of the manifold grace of God" (1 Pet. 4:10).
- "Encourage one another and build up one another, just as you also are doing" (1 Thess. 5:11).

- "Be devoted to one another in brotherly love; give preference to one another in honor; not lagging behind in dili-
gence, fervent in spirit, serving the Lord; rejoicing in hope,
persevering in tribulation, devoted to prayer, contributing
to the needs of the saints, practicing hospitality" (Rom.
12:10–13).

- "Do not complain, brethren, against one another, so that
you yourselves may not be judged; behold, the Judge is
standing right at the door" (James 5:9).

- "Let us not judge one another anymore, but rather determine this—not to put an obstacle or a stumbling block in
a brother's way" (Rom. 14:13).

- "Bear one another's burdens, and thereby fulfill the law of
Christ" (Gal. 6:2).

How does it sound to live in a community founded on loving
one another? Can you imagine the joy of lifelong friends who
are dedicated to serving and encouraging one another? Can you
imagine a place where people give preference to one another and
don't complain about one another? A place where people refuse
to judge one another but instead choose to bear one another's
burdens through mutual support?

That's the family of God. That's the blessing we're called to create
as Jesus followers, and that's the community we're invited to enjoy.

### Practical Steps

Maybe you're thinking, *All that sounds great. I'm thankful I get
to be part of God's family. But how do I make all this happen?
What are my responsibilities?*

We'll explore these and other practical questions as we move through this section of the book. But one thing you need to remember is that you can't "do" anything to make such a community happen. The kind of community I've been describing can't possibly be created by people through their own strength. This isn't the type of family or community we experience naturally when we're left to ourselves.

When we seek to participate in the community of God's family, the community itself is the result of Jesus's life and presence overflowing through our lives. Remember, the life of a Jesus follower begins by intentionally pursuing Christ and cultivating a relationship with Him (Abide). And when that happens, Jesus brings us into His family. It's through His presence and power in our lives that we participate in and maintain relationships with others as His church (Connect).

We can't live out the New Testament's "one another" admonitions and encouragements on our own. Only as Christ in us lives through us can we relate to one another the way God intends. But the wonderful outcome is that, as we allow Christ in us to shape our "one another" relationships, God uses those relationships to deepen and grow our love relationship with Him.

That's the miracle of life in God's family.

# 7

# Freedom from Relational Conflict

> Everything that comes as a barrier between us and
> another, be it ever so small, comes as a barrier between
> us and God.
>
> Roy Hession

For many years, the Martinez and Dominguez families lived in peace next to each other in their San Antonio, Texas, neighborhood. They visited each other's homes, and one Dominguez family member even attended the wedding of his neighbors' daughter.

Then came a change. The families disagree on exactly what happened, but it seems the Dominguez family posted recipes for juices on Facebook after getting into juicing as part of seeking a healthier lifestyle. When members of the Martinez family tried the juices, they didn't like them—and they made their opinions known online.

For most neighbors, such a minor dispute might create hurt feelings for a few days. At worst, it might be the end of a friendship. For the Martinez and Dominguez families, however, it prompted a much darker period.

In the years after that initial dispute, the Martinez family built a four-foot-tall wooden fence between their properties, and then the Dominguez family countered with a twelve-foot-tall barrier made of wood and corrugated metal. Then both families set up surveillance cameras. At one point, the Dominguez family alone had more than twenty cameras installed.

The feud really heated up when the Dominguezes' trash cans kept getting knocked over. They claimed the Martinez clan was using cattle prods to blast the cans over and knock out the contents. Then paintings of pigs appeared on the side of the fence facing the Martinez home, and that family accused the Dominguez family of not only painting them but of their patriarch making pig noises whenever a member of the Martinez family left their house.

All told, at the time of this report in 2015, San Antonio police officers had been sent to both homes roughly 140 times to address disputes or respond to accusations. Both families had sued. They all said they wanted to bring the feud to an end, but of course their preferred solution was for the other family to move away.[1]

Now, I've never elevated a neighborhood quarrel to the level of building a twelve-foot fence and installing surveillance cameras all over my yard—and I hope the same is true of you. But I know relational stress and strain are common in today's world. We all experience it at one level or another.

That includes our relationships within the church.

Fortunately, as we intentionally abide in Christ and seek out a deeper relationship with Him, He will allow His goodness to overflow through our lives and into our relationships with others. And in doing so, we can find freedom from relational pain.

## The Burden of Conflict

What causes conflict and quarrels within the church? It's funny you should ask, because the apostle James asked that very question as he wrote his epistle to the earliest Christians. Thankfully, he also gave us an answer:

> What is the source of quarrels and conflicts among you? Is not the source your pleasures that wage war in your members? You lust and do not have; so you commit murder. You are envious and cannot obtain; so you fight and quarrel. You do not have because you do not ask. You ask and do not receive, because you ask with wrong motives, so that you may spend it on your pleasures. You adulteresses, do you not know that friendship with the world is hostility toward God? Therefore whoever wishes to be a friend of the world makes himself an enemy of God. (James 4:1–4)

As we read this passage, we need to remember that James was writing to Christians—in his words, to his "brethren" (1:2). So the negative stuff he described in these verses wasn't directed outside the church but inside. He was addressing problems experienced by fellow Jesus followers.

If we're honest, we have to admit we see the same problems at work within the church today. Right? We believe something will bring us pleasure, and we do whatever is necessary to get it. We wish we had the success or the position or the influence of someone else within our congregation, and so we envy that person. We lust for what we believe will make us happy or satisfied or secure, and we quarrel over whatever that is. And when we do bring God into the equation, asking Him for what we wish we had or for characteristics we wish we could demonstrate, we make our request with selfish rather than godly motives.

James identified our human sinfulness as the core of our relational conflict—even within the church. We cause one another pain and feel insulted and hold grudges because of "friendship" with the world. Meaning, we think and act with the same sinful and selfish patterns as those who have never encountered Christ.

Now, you might wonder, *How can Christians behave in these ways and not realize what they're doing? How are we at the point where there's all this division and strain within the church and yet we don't always seem to realize it's there?*

In my experience, one of the main answers to these questions is the same root issue we've been exploring throughout this book— we experience conflict within the church when we try to live out of our own resources rather than allowing Christ to live His life through us. Loving people is hard work. Loving people sacrificially, the way Christ loves us and the way He has commanded us to love one another, is impossible in our own strength.

Another issue develops when we try to navigate relationships within the church out of our own resources. Specifically, we've become good at covering our selfishness with a blanket of spirituality. Or, more accurately, we cover our conflict-causing thoughts and actions with a blanket of religion.

Here's how it works. We've already established that "religion" is when I try to use a system of rules and regulations to maintain control over my spiritual life, perhaps to keep score in a way that ensures I'm always in the lead. These systems are how many people within the church determine what a "good Christian" should be.

The problem is that different people have different sets of rules and regulations they think are most important, different lists for what a "good Christian" looks like. Therefore, when you do things I believe are wrong according to my list, and when I don't do what's essential according to your list, we're bound to be in conflict.

Basically, one driver of quarrels and conflicts within the church is that people have strong opinions about why their "religion" is best. And the same principle exists on a larger scale as well. Entire groups within the church constantly squabble and snipe because they all think their rules are the *right* rules and everyone else should conform to their definition of what it means to live as a Jesus follower.

As a pastor, I can tell you from direct experience that the conflict and strain we experience within the church create a heavy burden. I've seen marriages torn apart, which creates a weight not just for a husband and wife to carry but for their children, friends, and extended families to carry. And I've seen congregations split over which songs are most worshipful, how many services should be available on Sunday mornings, how to allocate the church missions budget, and other seemingly insignificant points of conflict. That creates a burden not only for the members of the congregation but for the entire community.

But perhaps the worst examples of relational conflict and strain occur when there is no split—no separation. Instead, church members dig their trenches like soldiers in World War I. People continue to meet for worship or their Sunday school class or their small group, but an underlying layer of hostility exists. Of stubborn pride. Of believing *I'm right and you're wrong, and this situation can be resolved only when you bend your knee and admit that victory is mine.*

That kind of conflict creates an incredible burden—a weight we were never meant to carry within the family of God.

### The First Steps toward Freedom

I have good news and bad news when it comes to finding freedom from relational conflict within the church.

The good news is that you can find freedom. You can experience what it's like for that burden of conflict to be removed. You don't have to continue pretending everything's okay when you see "that person" or "those people" week after week, year after year. You don't have to continue being boiled alive in the slowly simmering heat of a conflict so old you don't even remember how it started. You don't have to keep carrying the anger or the bitterness or the resentment—or even the guilt.

You can let all that go. You can be set free from those burdens caused by relational strife. That's the good news.

The bad news is that the good news starts with you. You need to take the first step. Or, as we'll see below, you need to take the first steps, plural.

We've already talked about the need to let go of religion and embrace the simplicity of a relationship with Jesus. As I've mentioned, religion is a major underlying factor in the quarrels and strife that exist within the church. For that reason, the best thing you can do is reject the temptation to judge everything and everyone by your specific opinions of what makes a good Christian. Instead, choose to abide in your relationship with Christ, and then He'll give you opportunities to establish and enjoy meaningful relationships with others—relationships that won't include the burden and baggage of religion.

So that's the first step: let go of religion. The next step often feels much more difficult.

In Romans 12:18, the apostle Paul writes these challenging words: "If possible, so far as it depends on you, be at peace with all men." Wow. Several commands in the Bible are difficult to wrap my mind around, but this is among the top ones. Be at peace with all people. With everyone. All the time.

This verse can be difficult to live out for two reasons. First, Paul included an important qualifier—"so far as it depends on you"—but sometimes making a wrong right and bringing peace to a relationship is beyond your control. When you do the right thing by humbling yourself and seeking forgiveness in the middle of a quarrel, your actions might not be received or reciprocated.

The second reason is that you don't always know when you've wronged someone. Not long ago, I wronged someone, but I was unaware I had.

As churches grow and change, team members can change too. One leader who transitioned off our team settled in one of our church plants in the city, but at the time, I didn't realize how poorly I had pastored him and his family through their time of transition. It's not that I didn't want to do a good job helping them, but I was distracted by other things, and I failed. Even worse, I had no idea I had hurt them—let alone had any knowledge of the deep level of their pain.

Several months later, their pastor approached me privately and told me about the wound I'd created. As soon as he finished talking, the Holy Spirit deeply convicted me. I'm so thankful for a brother willing to bring this issue to my attention and challenge me to pursue reconciliation.

That same afternoon, I rearranged my schedule to contact the man I had offended. I didn't want another day to go by without apologizing. We talked, I apologized, and I asked his forgiveness. Graciously, he received my apology and forgave me.

Imagine what would have happened if my pride had been in the way. What if I had talked myself out of apologizing for the harm I'd caused? *I'm the senior pastor here. I can't show weakness to the other staff! I can't let them think I'm less spiritual than they are.*

If I had allowed my pride to take over and refused to apologize, I would have created a situation that would have eventually led to major burdens. I would have caused strain between the other pastor and me. I would have aggravated the wound my former staff member suffered. I probably would have created stress between my wife and me, because I'm sure I would have told her what was going on, and I'm sure she would have seen the need for me to repent. And I certainly would have caused stress in my relationship with God by ignoring the conviction of His Holy Spirit.

That's a lot of burdens! And that's why I'm so thankful for the privilege of letting those burdens go and finding freedom in my relationships with others.

**Reality #2:** *It's impossible to be right with God if I'm not right with God's family.*

We've focused a few times on John 14:15, where Jesus says, "If you love Me, you will keep My commandments." Again, this isn't Jesus saying, "If you love Me, you better obey Me." Rather, the emphasis is on loving Jesus first, resulting in obedience second. This is Jesus saying, "If you love Me, obedience will spill out of your life."

Now let's take a look at how Jesus built on this teaching in the next chapter of John's Gospel: "This is My commandment, that you love one another, just as I have loved you" (15:12). This is Jesus's most direct phrasing of a point He made throughout His public ministry. He was saying the first evidence of my being in a right relationship with God is showing love to God's family. Or stated in another way, if I truly love Jesus, He will prove that love in me by helping me love the other members of God's family.

I like to combine John 14:15 and John 15:12: "If you love Me, you will keep My commandments" [and] "this is My commandment, that you love one another, just as I have loved you."

That brings us to Reality #2. In the previous chapter, I mentioned that there are three realities that express themselves in the life of a Jesus follower when our relationship with Him overflows into a relationship with others in the church. The first reality is this: *Because I have a relationship with God, I now have a relationship with God's family.*

And now here's Reality #2: *It's impossible to be right with God if I'm not right with God's family.*

Don't miss the importance of this reality—this truth. As you pursue intimacy with Christ (Abide), His life begins pressing out through your life. His love and power flow into you and through you so they can make a difference for His kingdom. And the first obvious evidence of His life in you is your love for your brothers and sisters in Christ (Connect). You can't have one without the other. It's impossible. Now, this doesn't mean your love for others in God's family is the *only* expression of Jesus living His life through you, but it will be the first expression.

Let me say this as plainly as I can. If you want to know whether you're walking in right relationship with God, the first question to ask yourself is, *Am I actively showing love to my brothers and sisters in Christ?* If answering this question reveals something isn't right between you and a brother or sister in Christ, then something isn't right between you and God.

And if that's the case, you need to seek reconciliation.

*Reconciliation* is a beautiful term. It means bringing together those who are separate. Our world needs reconciliation across racial, cultural, and geopolitical lines—overcoming obstacles. And as followers of Jesus, we know true reconciliation is possible only through the power of the gospel.

Here's what Paul said about our role in this process of reconciliation: "Now all these things are from God, who reconciled us to Himself through Christ and gave us the ministry of reconciliation, namely, that God was in Christ reconciling the world to Himself, not counting their trespasses against them, and He has committed to us the word of reconciliation" (2 Cor. 5:18–19).

From this passage, we understand that the gospel first provides reconciliation on a vertical level. Meaning, we can experience reconciliation between ourselves and God. Obviously, that's crucial. We weren't right with God by nature, but what Jesus did through His death, burial, and resurrection has made it possible for us to be made right with God. The gospel offers this ministry of reconciliation—and thank God!

But the reconciliation taking place through the power of the gospel isn't just vertical; it's also horizontal. Now that we're reconciled with God through Christ, we've also been reconciled in our relationships with one another as brothers and sisters in Christ. And the way I know I've experienced reconciliation vertically is that I've enjoyed reconciliation horizontally.

Here's a challenging message from 1 John 4:20–21: "If someone says, 'I love God,' and hates his brother, he is a liar; for the one who does not love his brother whom he has seen, cannot love God whom he has not seen. And this commandment we have from Him, that the one who loves God should love his brother also."

I know what you might be thinking. *Well, I don't* hate *my brothers and sisters in Christ. I'd just rather not be around some of them.* Before you justify your position, understand the meaning of that word *hate*. In the Greek language, it means "ill feelings that affect the way you act toward someone."[2] So, practically, here's what this means for you: if you have resentment, bitterness, anger, unforgiveness, or any other ill feeling in your heart toward a brother or sister in Christ, and you're parading around like everything between you and God is good, you're lying to yourself and lying to the people around you.

The Scriptures are clear. It's a lie to say we're right with God if we're not right with someone in His family.

**The Highest Standard**

So what are you supposed to do if you're carrying anger or resentment or bitterness or any other ill feeling toward a fellow member of God's family? Jesus gave you the answer: "If you are presenting your offering at the altar, and there remember that your brother has something against you, leave your offering there before the altar and go; first be reconciled to your brother, and then come and present your offering" (Matt. 5:23–24).

Try to imagine that scenario. You're in the middle of worship on Sunday morning. God is moving. The Word is being preached. People are worshiping, singing, praising, and giving testimony. And then the Holy Spirit of God whispers to you in your spirit: *something between you and your brother* (or sister) *in Christ is not right.*

In that moment, Jesus says, "Stop what you're doing. Leave the altar of worship. Go and make things right. Be reconciled to your brother, and then come back to church and worship God." Once again, Jesus makes it plain that it's impossible to be in a right posture of worship toward God if you're not in right relationship with your brother or sister in God's family.

One of the most powerful books I've read on this subject—informing the way I relate to my brothers and sisters in Christ—is titled *The Calvary Road*. Its author is Roy Hession. Here's something Roy writes that really captures the heart of what I want you to understand from this chapter:

> Everything that comes as a barrier between us and another, be it ever so small, comes as a barrier between us and God. . . . Our relationship with our fellows and our relationship with God are so linked that we cannot disturb one without disturbing the other.[3]

We're always indwelt by the Holy Spirit, but I believe a unique manifestation of the Holy Spirit of God occurs when we come together and worship as God's people. I also believe that manifest presence of the Holy Spirit is squelched when brothers and sisters in Christ go through the motions of worshiping God while brokenness remains in their relationships with one another.

If you're not sure about that, look back at John 15:12 to see how Jesus raised the bar even higher. He said we're to "love one another, just as I have loved you." Did you catch that? *Just as I have loved you.* What a standard! Think about all the ways Jesus has expressed His love for you. He loves you sacrificially and unconditionally. He loves you faithfully. He loves you patiently. He loves you with a love that never runs dry or lessens or fades even a single degree.

Maybe you're thinking, *There's no way! I can't love like that.* And in one sense, you're exactly right. In our own strength, we can't love like that. But remember, Christianity is not you and me living for Jesus in our own strength. Christianity is Jesus living in and through us out of the overflow of an abiding relationship with Him. So to the degree that we pursue intimacy with Christ and Christ begins to live through us, we have the capacity to love our brothers and sisters in Christ just as Christ has loved us.

Once again, the focus here is not on feeling pressure to prove your love for your brothers and sisters in Christ. The focus is on loving Jesus and allowing Him to love our brothers and sisters in Christ through us. That's the simplicity and freedom of following Jesus.

Speaking of simplicity, don't forget that Jesus's words throughout this chapter are commands, not suggestions. If you realize conflict exists between you and another member of God's family, He commands you to make it right. And when you interact with your brothers and sisters in Christ, He commands you to love them just as He loves you.

Some people don't like the idea of being commanded—even by God. But in my mind, a wonderful simplicity comes with being a Jesus follower, especially in terms of dealing with relational strife. That's because the pressure to figure things out is no longer on me. I don't have to ask myself, *Is he really sorry?* Or, *Does she deserve an apology?* Or, *Is this the right time to try to patch up this relationship?* My Lord and Savior has told me what I need to do and when I need to do it. And that's not a burden of any kind. That's the simplicity and freedom of following Jesus.

## The Blessing of Unity

We've seen that living as a Jesus follower brings freedom from the burden of relational strife by leading us to deal with quarrels and conflict rather than leaving wounds to fester. But it's also important to recognize that living as a Jesus follower should reduce the amount of relational strife we experience in the first place.

I made the case earlier that living in our own strength causes conflict within the church. It leads to each person following his or her opinions about what it means to faithfully follow Christ. But that's not how the church is supposed to operate. We're supposed to demonstrate unity as the family of God.

In the letter known as 1 Corinthians, the apostle Paul writes to a church that had been fractured by different forms of religion. Here's what he says: "I have been informed concerning you, my brethren, by Chloe's people, that there are quarrels among you. Now I mean this, that each one of you is saying, 'I am of Paul,' and 'I of Apollos,' and 'I of Cephas,' and 'I of Christ.' Has Christ been divided? Paul was not crucified for you, was he? Or were you baptized in the name of Paul?" (1 Cor. 1:11–13).

Different groups within this one regional church had their own ideas of what it meant to be a "true Christian." Some people thought Paul was the right person to model as a Jesus follower. Others wanted to model themselves after Apollos or Cephas (Peter). And still others had the correct idea—following Christ.

We might read those words today and shake our heads in confusion. *How could a single church have that many divisions?* But maybe we need to take another look at the condition of our own churches and our own expression of the body of Christ. Today, the body as a whole is as fractured as it's ever been. Like the Corinthians, many of us have a skewed "ideal" of what it means to follow Jesus. Some of us attach that ideal to a political party. Some of us attach it to celebrities—including celebrities who are also Jesus followers. Some of us attach it to pastors or authors or our neighbors down the street.

Thankfully, the solution is the same today as it was during Paul's time. Here's what he told the Corinthians—and us: "Now I exhort you, brethren, by the name of our Lord Jesus Christ, that you all agree and that there be no divisions among you, but that you be made complete in the same mind and in the same judgment" (1 Cor. 1:10).

What was Paul's answer? Unity. He exhorted the Corinthians to "agree" and bring themselves together "in the same mind." You might think, *How in the world can that happen today? There's no way to get all these different groups within the church to agree on what's "best."*

And that's certainly true. There's no way for us to wrangle everyone in the church together and find a consensus for what's the "right" way to follow Jesus. But why would we want to do that? That's still following a religion through our own resources. That's still strapping a burden to our backs and trying to convince everyone we have the "right" burden. No thank you.

The way to find unity within the church is for each of us to cast off religion and turn back to our relationship with Jesus. As we abide in Him, He will fill us with Himself. And as Jesus's own life overflows through us and into our relationships within the church, He will lead us all in the direction we should go.

**When You've Been Hurt by the Church**

Before I conclude this section, I'd like to say something to those who've had a bad experience within the church, to those who've been hurt.

First, let me say this: I understand. I really do understand what you've experienced and how you've been wounded. As I mentioned in the introduction, I've been around churches my entire life, and I've experienced a lot in those churches that's caused me pain. I've been wounded by my church as a member, and I've been wounded by my church as a pastor. It's real, and it hurts. I understand.

The second thing I want to say is this: isolating yourself from the church will never heal those wounds. Never. Removing yourself from community or refusing to fellowship with the church is not the answer.

Please hear me; we don't have the right to throw out the biblical concept of community just because relationships can be challenging and difficult. In His infinite wisdom, God has given us His Word as a guidebook. And in the Bible, it's clear that He designed us for community—not only to bless us as individuals but to bless the world through our relationships, including by how we forgive one another.

You know those nature shows on the Discovery Channel, where in one scene a lion is prowling low in the grass, sneaking up on a herd of gazelles? One gazelle is always off by itself, away from the herd. How does it turn out for that one gazelle out there all alone? Two words for you: *not good*.

In one of his epistles to the church, the apostle Peter made it clear that we have an enemy as Jesus followers. He said, "Be of sober spirit, be on the alert. Your adversary, the devil, prowls around like a roaring lion, seeking someone to devour" (1 Pet. 5:8). As Christians, our enemy is prowling around like a roaring lion, seeking someone to devour. And if you're the one who drifts off by yourself, apart from community with others, it's not good.

# 8

# Freedom from Isolation

We should not . . . think of our fellowship with other Christians as a spiritual luxury, an optional addition to the exercises of private devotion. We should recognize rather that such fellowship is a spiritual necessity; for God has made us in such a way that our fellowship with Him is fed by our fellowship with fellow Christians, and requires to be so fed constantly for its own deepening and enrichment.

J. I. Packer

In March 2016, college student Kelsey Harmon joined her grandfather, whom she calls Papaw, at his house for dinner. Kelsey was expecting some or all of her cousins to be at the dinner as well, but all five had other commitments.

As a joke, Kelsey snapped a photo of her grandpa looking sad and holding a hamburger. Then she posted the photo online with this message: "Dinner with papaw tonight . . . He made 12 burgers for all 6 grandkids and I'm the only one who showed. love him."[1] The photo was especially pitiful, with Papaw looking down at the table, looking forlorn.

Unbeknownst to either Kelsey or her grandfather, that moment was the start of one of the more popular internet memes in history. Kelsey's photo went viral, with millions of views across the internet in the first few days. People from all over the world commented on the image—some sending their love and support to "Sad Papaw," others expressing their desire to have one more meal with their own departed grandparents, and even others scolding Kelsey's five cousins for making Pawpaw feel sad.

With most memes, this massive response would have been an interesting end to the story, the attention fizzling after a few days. But not for Papaw, whose name is Kenneth Harmon. Both surprised and delighted by the outpouring of support, Harmon was especially moved by the people who said they would love to join him for a burger. What did he do? He invited them to his house!

About two weeks after the initial photo was posted, Papaw (and the rest of his grandchildren) hosted a cookout with an open invitation for anyone to come and "have a burger with Papaw." Harmon even sold T-shirts at the event that read, "I ate a burger with Sad Papaw." In the end, hundreds of people responded to the invitation, some traveling for more than twenty hours to participate.[2]

Ultimately, the story of Sad Papaw is uplifting rather than depressing. But for many people throughout the world—including many within the church—loneliness and isolation are realities of everyday life that don't have a happy ending.

## The Burden of Isolation

With each passing year, people in America seem to become more and more isolated. In fact, I was shocked when I read an article recently about a new study that found that half of Americans are lonely. According to that article, 54 percent of adults said they always or sometimes felt like no one knew them well. Similarly, 40 percent of the respondents said they felt like they "lack[ed] companionship," their "relationships [weren't] meaningful," and they were "isolated from others."[3]

One other finding I found surprising was that younger adults experience more isolation and loneliness than those in older generations. A measurement called the UCLA Loneliness Scale rates a person's loneliness on a scale from 20 to 80. According to the study, people from Generation Z (those born between the mid-1990s and the early 2000s) had an overall loneliness score of 48.3. Millennials had a score of 45.3. But people aged 72 and above had an average score of 38.6.[4]

These numbers and themes are concerning. And they're not just concerning for younger people; they're concerning for us all. Even with technology and social media, we're becoming more and more isolated as a culture. As we find cures for diseases and make progress with helping others in need, we're becoming more and more lonely. Even as the global population skyrockets year after year, we're separated from one another at a higher rate than ever before.

Most importantly, these numbers should concern us because of what we've already seen from Scripture—it's "not good" for us to be alone. We're created in the image of God, who is a relational Being. Therefore, anything that makes us more isolated from one another also pulls us farther away from Him.

Isolation is a major burden in the lives of many people. Loneliness is too. These are social problems, yes, but they are also spiritual problems. And that means we need spiritual solutions.

Thankfully, God's design for His church is the perfect cure for isolation. As we turn to Jesus and abide with Him, He will lead us together as the body of Christ. And the more we come together, the more we'll experience freedom from the burdens of loneliness and isolation.

**Reality #3:** *My relationship with God grows by fellowship with His family.*

Beyond avoiding isolation and loneliness is another compelling reason for us to seek the community God has provided through the church: our own spiritual growth.

Already, we've identified two important realities we will experience as we come together in biblical community. Reality #1 is because I have a relationship with God, I now have a relationship with God's family. Reality #2 is it's impossible to be right with God if I'm not right with God's family.

Now here's Reality #3: *My relationship with God grows by fellowship with His family.*

Here's the big picture: my relationship with God is what enables me to fully enjoy my relationship with others. *But* my relationship with others is what God uses to deepen my relationship with Him. Our spiritual growth and progression through the Abide and Connect relationships is a cycle.

You see, making this personal, because I know Jesus, by grace I've been given this incredible relationship with my brothers and sisters in Christ. But it's my relationship with them that deepens and grows my fellowship relationship with God. These relationships are interdependent. As Christians, we can genuinely say this to one another: "I have you because I have Him, and I grow to know Him more because I have you."

Here's another way to express this truth: we will never learn some things about God apart from relationships with other believers. That's certainly been the case in my life, and I'm confident the same has been true for you.

Let me explain. I didn't learn some things about myself until I got married. Why? Because until then, no one had been as close to me and willing to tell me the absolute truth about myself. Right? Spouses can say things to each other no one else can.

For example, sometimes when I'm in a conversation, I assume I already know what the other person is going to say. So I jump in and cut them off. Apparently, I've done this for much of my life. But because of the relational equity and intimacy I enjoy with my wife, she took the initiative to talk about it with me. One morning she sat down next to me and said, "Hon, do you know you cut off people when they're talking? It's kind of—"

"Baby, I don't do that. What are you talking about?"

Evidently, I needed to make a change in my conversations with others, but I couldn't see it myself. I needed someone walking close enough to me to lovingly point it out.

I also never could have discovered some truths about the world without my wife. For example, having grown up in the southeastern United States, I didn't know pinto beans, cornbread, and fried potatoes went together so well. That was a truth I needed to discover! But to come to that discovery, I had to be around somebody else.

On a more serious note, God desires to work out many changes in our character. He's at work accomplishing His purpose of conforming us to the image of Christ. Also, He wants us to know truths about Him so we can grow in our understanding of Him.

Some areas of our walk need to be sharpened, but if we just pop into church for a couple of hours each week with our *I'm doing great* church smiles on our faces, we're never going to experience the kind of transformation God wants for us.

The author of Hebrews gave an important challenge on this theme:

> Let us hold fast the confession of our hope without wavering, for He who promised is faithful; and let us consider how to stimulate one another to love and good deeds, not forsaking our own assembling together, as is the habit of some, but encouraging one another; and all the more as you see the day drawing near. (Heb. 10:23–25)

That passage says we need to "stimulate" one another to love and good deeds. Other Bible translations use the word *spur*—almost like we prod each other forward toward spiritual growth. It's not always a comfortable experience, but it's necessary if we want the full measure of growth God has for us. And it's worth the effort.

When you experience real community and enjoy your relationship with God in fellowship with other believers, God uses those relationships to accomplish His activity in your life. (And get this—He uses you to accomplish His activity in others' lives too.) Through relationships with others, He conforms us to His image. He reveals truths about who He is. He sharpens and shapes our walk. He invites us to join in His activity.

All this happens in the context of community. And all this helps us find not just growth but freedom from the burden of isolation.


### The Importance of Small Groups

Earlier, I mentioned my first experiences with an "accountability group," which didn't go over so well for me. But I don't want to give the impression that small groups are unhelpful—or even that I abandoned smaller groups of community after that first taste. Far from it.

I've personally been a part of small-group communities with other believers for more than twenty-five years. Doing life together with followers of Jesus has challenged and deepened my relationship with God in ways I never could have imagined. The words of encouragement, the testimonies, the prayers, the caring from others have revolutionized my understanding of who God is and transformed my personal love relationship with Him.

The Bible describes this process with some interesting imagery in Proverbs 27:17: "Iron sharpens iron, so one man sharpens another." In ancient times, people sharpened dulled iron tools or weapons by bringing them together. The same thing happens spiritually in a community of believers—we sharpen one another.

Unfortunately, many in the church have diminished the idea of fellowship to merely mean "coffeepots and casseroles." However, the biblical concept of fellowship is much deeper. The New Testament word most often translated as "fellowship" is the Greek word *koinonia*. This word means "to share in the life of another."[5] That's why people in small-group ministries often talk about "doing life together."

Here's an important question: Do you have fellow believers in your life with whom you can "do life together"? Do you have brothers and sisters in Christ who are walking closely with you as you all learn what it means to faithfully follow Jesus? Do you know people who challenge you in that walk, help you discover new truths, and lead you deeper in your love relationship with God? Do others lean on you for these benefits as well?

I hope so. Being in a group is more than just participating in another church program. It's not just one more thing you're supposed to do to be a good Christian. Enjoying a deeper level of biblical fellowship is part of the plan God designed for anyone who wants to live as a Jesus follower.

That's been true since the earliest versions of the church: "They were continually devoting themselves to the apostles' teaching and to fellowship, to the breaking of bread and to prayer. . . . Day by day continuing with one mind in the temple, and breaking bread from house to house" (Acts 2:42, 46).

Speaking of Acts 2, it's important to note again that nobody had to show the early believers how to form these communities. It happened organically. Once they came to Christ, they immediately joined together with others who had also experienced Him. Nobody said, "Okay, here's the program. We're going to organize a small-groups ministry." No. They just started living out their new relationship with God as a family. They did it together because that's exactly how God designed life to work.

### Fellowship and Mission

Yet many people *want* to live the Christian life on their own. When I talk with those who feel that way, they often ask, "Why is it such a big deal if I don't feel like going to church? Why is it a problem if I don't want to join a group or get established in some community?"

Well, as we've seen, the first reason is personal to those people as individuals. They'll never know God's best for them apart from fellowship with His children. They'll never develop the spiritual depth and maturity God planned for them if they separate themselves from other believers who can help them grow.

But fellowship is so important for an even bigger reason, and this reason is missional. The world will never know God apart from seeing the fellowship of believers. During the Last Supper, Jesus made that clear to His disciples—and to us: "A new commandment I give to you, that you love one another, even as I have loved you, that you also love one another. By this all men will know that you are My disciples, if you have love for one another" (John 13:34–35).

You see, God's plan is that our relationships with one another be so powerful—so transformational and undeniable—that they reveal Jesus to the world. It's His plan that people outside the church see our love for and devotion to one another and be drawn to Jesus.

One of the terms for the church in the Bible is *the body of Christ*. Here's how the apostle Paul introduced that concept:

> Even as the body is one and yet has many members, and all the members of the body, though they are many, are one body, so also is Christ. For by one Spirit we were all baptized into one body, whether Jews or Greeks, whether slaves or free, and we were all made to drink of one Spirit. . . . Now you are Christ's body, and individually members of it. (1 Cor. 12:12–13, 27)

This is a crucial truth. People need to see and understand that Jesus Christ is still accomplishing His work in this world. He's no longer in His former body, which was crucified and resurrected, but He's still here. And He's still at work through the body of Christ, the church.

Think of it this way: How do you know Vance Pitman is real? Because I have a body. You can see me. How will the world know God is real? They must see His body. And *we* are His body. As we live in fellowship with one another, as we love one another, as we serve one another, as we do life together, and as we care for one another, the world sees the body of Christ.

By God's design, in response to our fellowship with one another, the world should say, "Jesus must be real, because we can
see Him in His followers."

John taught this principle in his first letter to the church, which
we know as the book of 1 John. He said, "No one has seen God
at any time; if we love one another, God abides in us, and His love
is perfected in us" (4:12). John said no one has seen God. But as
we love one another, He abides in us, and the world sees Christ.
That's why Jesus said, "By this all men will know that you are My
disciples, if you have love for one another" (John 13:35).

Following Jesus is about a love relationship with God. But following Jesus is also about a love relationship with your brothers
and sisters in Christ. Do these principles describe your experience of following Jesus? Genuine fellowship, authentic community,
doing life together—this is the life of a Jesus follower.

## We Can't Do It Alone

In the summer of 2018, I was in San Diego on a writing retreat.
As I walked through downtown with a friend, we came to an intersection, and I noticed a man in a wheelchair with a couple of
grocery sacks in his lap. From his clothing, I got the impression
he was a veteran of the US military.

When the light changed, he wheeled himself off the curb, but
the intersection was on a steep grade. He made it about a third of
the way before he began to roll backward. My friend and I started
to react, but before we could move very far, a young man quickly
jumped in to help, assisting the man in the wheelchair all the way
through the intersection.

As my friend and I walked away, I said, "What if that guy had
been alone? What would he have done?"

I'm not exactly sure why this moment struck me as deeply as it did, but it reinforced to me the truth that, as Christians, we can't live the life of a Jesus follower on our own. We need others in our lives. And we especially need others to help us navigate the downs of life.

All of us walk through moments of celebration and joy, but we also walk through moments of sorrow and pain. God has united us as a family so we never have to tackle those moments alone. That's the beauty of being part of God's family. That's the gift of being freed forever from the burden of isolation.

Let's go back to Acts 2, to the story about the birth of Christian community known as the church: "All those who had believed were together and had all things in common; and they began selling their property and possessions and were sharing them with all, as anyone might have need" (vv. 44–45). Notice the passage says they "were together." These two little words give us a powerful reality: these new Christians enjoyed a constant state of being together.

But pay careful attention to what happened next. The Bible doesn't tell us exactly how it happened, but we know these Jesus followers were doing life together when they became aware people in the family had needs. And let me tell you what they didn't do. They didn't say, "Well, good luck with that." They didn't say, "Wow, I hope you find the resources to take care of that, because it's awful." They didn't say, "Hey, you should let one of the apostles know about this need." And they didn't even say, "I'll ask God to meet that need for you."

According to the Bible, those early believers went into action. They did whatever was necessary to meet one another's needs.

You see, this is another amazing dynamic of being in God's family—we have a community of believers to meet our needs. That's exactly what happened in Acts 2. The members of the church sold their property and possessions and shared what they had with those in need. That's incredibly powerful! That's radical generosity! That's *really* loving one another. That's Christian community.

Today we think this story is extreme and that it was a special time at the beginning of the church, but we don't need to meet that same standard now. But those early Jesus followers were being the church God designed the church to be.

Every one of us knows what it is to need something. Sometimes our need is financial. Sometimes it's emotional. Sometimes it's physical. Sometimes it's spiritual. Need is a reality in life.

Time for a checkup. The following questions are designed to help you discern whether you're walking with your brothers and sisters in Christ through life's ups and downs or choosing to remain in isolation.

Reflect on these questions. As you do, ask the Holy Spirit what He would like to communicate to you in this moment.

- Are you meeting needs within the body of Christ?
- Are you aware of any current needs other followers of Jesus have that God has given you the ability to meet?
- Are you sensitive to the leadership of the Holy Spirit in pointing out the needs of those around you?
- Do you find joy in meeting the needs of others?
- When was the last time God used you to meet a specific need in the life of one of your brothers or sisters in Christ? Can you remember?
- When was the last time you can remember God meeting *your* need through a brother or sister in Christ?

One of the primary ways God uses us to meet the needs of others is through our spiritual gifts. He's given each one of His children supernatural empowerments intended to build up their brothers and sisters in Christ.

One of the places we see this taught in Scripture is 1 Peter 4:10: "As each one has received a special gift, employ it in serving one another as good stewards of the manifold grace of God." (This is yet another example of the "one another" relationship that exists between brothers and sisters in Christ.)

These spiritual gifts are exactly that: gifts. They were given to us through the grace of Jesus in our lives. But they weren't given for us to keep or hold on to. Our spiritual gifts were given to be used— and specifically, given to serve others within the church. We've been grace-gifted to meet the needs of others by serving them.

When you're rightly following Jesus, you see the church not as a place that exists only to meet your needs but as a community where Christ in you can meet the needs of others.

In the context of God's family are two categories of relationships: healthy and unhealthy. Healthy relationships are characterized by love, honesty, trust, encouragement, transparency, and peace. God uses healthy relationships in His family to grow us. They encourage us. They provide examples for us. They build us up. They speak truth into our lives. They hold us accountable. They admonish us. And in all these ways and many more, they deepen our love relationship with God and cultivate a greater intimacy with Him.

Some believers you're doing life with have probably come to mind, people God is using to spur you on in your relationship with Him. Take a moment right now to thank God for them by name. They're an essential ingredient for your spiritual growth and witness to the world.

But sometimes God uses difficult relationships to challenge us. Maybe some unhealthy relationships are coming to mind, and the last thing you want to do is thank God for them. Let's be honest, even in the context of Christian community, some relationships can be tough. They can be messy. Maybe sin has damaged them—or conflict, misunderstanding, a difficult circumstance. For whatever reason, we all have difficult relationships in God's family.

But you can still thank God for those relationships. By His infinite grace, He's using even these relationships to grow your relationship with Him.

Now, I'm not talking about abuse. I'm not talking about situations where you're being intentionally harmed in any way. There should be no tolerance for abuse or abusive relationships anywhere, especially in the church. If you're experiencing anything that feels abusive, take action. Talk with someone and find a way to get out.

That being said, every relationship in your life has been allowed by God. God can still use unhealthy relationships to deepen your relationship with Him.

Here's another insight from Roy Hession in *The Calvary Road*, centering on selfishness and pride:

> We shall have to see that the thing in us that reacts so sharply to another's selfishness and pride is simply our own selfishness and pride, which we are unwilling to sacrifice. We shall have to accept another's ways and doings as God's will for us and meekly bend the neck to all of God's providences. That does not mean we must accept another's selfishness as God's will for them—far from it—but only as God's will for us.[6]

Hession wasn't saying when others act wrongly toward me it's right for them. He was saying when others act wrongly toward me, God in His grace can use even their wrong actions to accomplish His right purpose of making me more like Jesus. That's just how big God is! This means when I refuse to pursue reconciliation with a brother or sister in Christ—even when I've been wronged—I'm not just rejecting them; I'm also rejecting what God desires to do in my life through them.

Hession went on to say this: "It is no use pretending we are broken before God if we are not broken in our attitude to those around us. God nearly always tests us through other people."[7] One of the reasons we need to be in community with others is that God uses our relationships in His family to deepen our love relationship with Him.

Let me say it again: don't remove yourself from the blessing of community within God's family. Don't allow yourself to be isolated, even for a moment. That's bondage. That's a burden. Instead, choose to live in the freedom of mutually beneficial love. Choose to embrace the blessing of connecting with God and connecting with others through the gift of God's family.

# PART 4

# SHARE

How lovely on the mountains
Are the feet of him who brings good news,
Who announces peace
And brings good news of happiness,
Who announces salvation,
And says to Zion, "Your God reigns!"
Listen! Your watchmen lift up their voices,
They shout joyfully together;
For they will see with their own eyes
When the LORD restores Zion.

Isaiah 52:7–8

# 9

## You Have a Mission

Why should anyone hear the Gospel twice, before
everyone has heard it once?

Oswald J. Smith

I'm a numbers guy. I enjoy comparing sets of numbers, digging
into statistics, and learning about percentages. I'm often in the
minority when it comes to enjoying numbers, and I know many
people out there are horrified at the idea of voluntarily spending
time exploring them, but it really can be interesting.

For example, have you ever thought about the difference between a million and a billion? In one sense, you could say there's
not much difference at all. Just one letter difference distinguishes
the two words. And if we were to put those words in terms of dollars, both a million and a billion sound pretty good. Even looking
at the numerals doesn't seem to make that much of a difference.

A billion dollars is $1,000,000,000—which is a really big number. But a million dollars also looks huge—$1,000,000. We know a billion is more than a million, but we wouldn't complain if we inherited either sum. Right?

In reality, though, there's a tremendous difference between a million and a billion. An incredible difference.

Let's say you were going to count from one to one million, adding one number every second. So "one . . . two . . . three . . . four . . ."—all the way up to a million. It would take you about eleven and a half days to count that high. That would be a terrible way to spend a couple of weeks, in my opinion, but it could be done. It's possible.

Now let's say you wanted to do the same thing with a billion. Do you know how long it would take for you to get to a billion if you added one numeral every second? Almost thirty-two years! That's the difference between a million and a billion—the difference between eleven and a half days and thirty-two years!

Here's another way to think about that difference. If you were to set aside $45,000 a year and never spend a penny of it, it would take you twenty-two years to finally accumulate a million dollars. That's a long time. (And that makes me even more confused about all the people who become millionaires in their lifetimes. How do they do it?)

But do you know how long it would take to accumulate a billion dollars on the same schedule and with the same $45,000 every year? Twenty-two thousand years! A billion is a thousand millions, which is an incredible number to try to wrap our minds around.[1]

I know you're wondering, *Why is he making a big deal about these numbers?* The answer is that I want us to think seriously about one specific number—a number that points to our responsibilities as Jesus followers in a world that's desperate for Him.

## How Can They Hear?

The number I want to share with you is staggering. I've even been staring at it. Or to be more accurate, I've been staring at different versions of it because it's constantly changing.

Here's the number: 7,639,475,027.

That's the total population of our world as I sit here right now—the total number of people living and breathing on this planet. Remember how big a billion is? And as I said, the number will be different by the time you read this, because the global population increases by roughly forty people every ten seconds.

As followers of Jesus, we need to understand that every number in that total of more than 7.6 billion represents a soul. A person. A human being. These individuals have been made in the image of God to enjoy a relationship with the One who made them. Boys and girls. Men and women. Teenagers. Grandparents. Moms and dads. Aunts and uncles. All these people are precious in the sight of God.

And here's the critical truth: every one of these 7,639,475,027 people will spend eternity somewhere. And in Romans 10:14, Paul wrote, "How can [people] call on [the Lord] to save them unless they believe in him? And how can they believe in him if they have never heard about him? And how can they hear about him unless someone tells them?" (NLT).

These are penetrating, powerful questions, because they force us to think about that staggering number. Each of those 7.6 billion people needs to hear the good news of the gospel to receive the free gift of salvation offered by Jesus Christ. But how will they call out to Christ unless they believe in Him? And how will they believe in Him unless they hear the good news about Him? And how will they hear the good news of the gospel unless someone tells them?

Again, every one of those 7.6 billion people will spend eternity somewhere, including you. Including your loved ones. Including your neighbors and the people on the highways as you drive to work each day. Including the people who voted the same way you did in the last election and those who voted for the other side. Including every single person in every single country across the globe.

Every person needs the gospel of Jesus Christ.

Let's dig a little deeper into our number, 7,639,475,027, focusing on approximately 1.6 billion of them. These are the people who've never heard they can have true life because of what Christ did for them. They don't know anything about the gospel. They don't know God loves them.[2] And if they wanted to hear the good news about Jesus, they'd first have to learn a completely different language because no witness is accessible in theirs.

Think about that. What if for you to become a Christian, the first thing you had to do was learn a completely new language? That's a sad reality, but sometimes we fall into the habit of dismissing people from other countries—and especially people from primitive cultures—because we think, *Well, I don't speak their language. I don't know those people. They don't live here.*

But think about how many times you heard about Jesus before you came to know Him. Think about how many church services you sat through, how many sermons you heard, or how many friends shared the good news of Jesus with you before you finally gave your life to Him.

Let's bring this even closer to home. My home.

I love the city I live in. Unlike the people who have no access to the gospel, the people in Las Vegas *do* have access. But they still may never have heard the gospel presented in a clear and compelling way. Or they may have rejected the gospel message.

Here's what keeps me up at night: Las Vegas has a population of just over 2.2 million. In the most recent census data, 92 percent of residents declared no relationship with Jesus.[3] So out of the 2.2 million people who live here, just over 2 million aren't followers of Jesus. That's 2 million people who would spend eternity separated from God in hell if they died today.

Maybe you hear that number and think, *Well of course. Las Vegas is Sin City.* But not so fast. Unfortunately, this is not just the reality for Las Vegas.

Studies show that between 90 and 95 percent of people in nearly every major city in the western United States aren't followers of Jesus.[4] But statistics like these aren't limited to this most unchurched region in America. There's an epidemic of lostness and unbelief all over America—and all over the planet. Billions of souls, whether across the street from you or somewhere else in the world, woke up this morning with no relationship with Jesus, many without even any knowledge of Him. They've never experienced the saving power of the gospel.

### What's the Plan?

I'm not hitting you with these numbers and realities to upset you, and I'm certainly not doing it to make you feel guilty. In my experience, guilt accomplishes nothing good, especially within the body of Christ. No, I'm walking through all this with you because I hope you'll understand the seriousness of our situation. But I also hope you'll get excited! Yes, it's alarming that so many people in our world are lost, but we have the answer!

So the real question here is this: *What's the plan?* We can clearly see the need, but what is God's plan to tell the world about the gospel? What's God's plan to tell your city?

The answer to these questions might surprise you, but here it is: *you are the plan!*

Let me say that one more time just to let it sink in: you are the plan. God's plan to tell the world about His love and the truth of the gospel is centered on everyone seeking to live as a Jesus follower. I've heard it said this way: the plan of God is that the whole church take the whole gospel to the whole world.[5]

That's the plan.

Again, think about your own encounters with the truth of the gospel. Did you know a Christian before you knew Christ? The overwhelming majority of Jesus followers today ultimately met Jesus after they met another Jesus follower. God almost exclusively uses other people to share the good news with those who need to hear it. The life of Christ demonstrated through God's people leads to others' understanding of how the gospel can change them.

God's plan is to reach people through reached people. That includes you and me. We are the plan.

Here's an example of what that plan can look like in real life. My friend Drew is an all-American guy. He played sports in both high school and college. He married his high school sweetheart. He started his own multimillion-dollar business. He has beautiful children.

Drew and I first met coaching flag football. Our first season together, we were coaching our daughters. Our team was terrible; we didn't score a single touchdown until halfway through the season. Even then, we were losing by more than four touchdowns when we finally did score, but everyone on our side cheered like we had just won the league championship. Parents ran up and down the sideline. Girls in football uniforms did cartwheels. Video cameras rolled like it was a red-carpet event. It was a moment I'll never forget.

That season of ups and downs with this girls' flag football team wove a friendship between Drew and me. Throughout that season, we had many conversations. Some of them trying to come up with miracle plays to somehow teach our girls the game of football, and others about much more serious topics having to do with the game of life. We talked about spiritual things, and I shared my personal story of coming to know Jesus.

When the next season rolled around, Drew and I found ourselves coaching on separate teams, this time coaching our sons. Then one night after practice, Drew walked straight toward me from the other side of the field about a hundred yards away. I could tell by the look on his face that we were about to have a serious conversation. The first words out of his mouth were, "Vance, man, I've known you for over a year. And you know me. I've got a great life. I've got a beautiful wife. I've got great kids. I've got a great job. I wouldn't trade anything in my life. But you've got something I don't have. And I'd really love to know what that is."

And right there on the ball field, I shared the gospel with Drew again. I unpacked the truth about God and how he could know Him personally. Drew said he'd need to give it some thought. To my surprise, a couple of weeks later, I received a handwritten note from Drew in the mail. He wrote, "Vance, I thought about what you said, and I want you to know that I've given my life to Jesus. I am now a follower of Christ."

Throughout this final section of the book, about the concept Share, we'll explore the truth that God has sent us into the world to accomplish His mission, so through Christ in us, our neighbors, people like Drew, and the nations—people like the 1.6 billion who've never heard the gospel—can know the truth about God and come to know Him personally.

As followers of Jesus, we've all been invited to share in His mission. This invitation isn't only for pastors or missionaries or radical evangelists. This mission is for every follower of Jesus as Christ lives His life in and through us. John 3:16 says, "God so loved the world," and that same God has given you a mission to reveal His love to the world.

God invited you into a relationship with Himself because He loves you. But He also invited you into a relationship with Himself because He loves the people around you and desires to make Himself known to them through you. But *how* does Jesus make Himself known to the world through you? Through me?

One of the ways is our embracing His Great Commission.

## The Great Commission

After Jesus's resurrection from the grave, He spent forty days appearing to His disciples in different ways and offering final teachings on how they should live as members of His kingdom. Near the end of that period, before He ascended back to heaven, Jesus challenged His followers with some powerful and poignant words. Today, we often refer to these words as the Great Commission.

Here's what Jesus said:

> All authority has been given to Me in heaven and on earth. Go therefore and make disciples of all the nations, baptizing them in the name of the Father and the Son and the Holy Spirit, teaching them to observe all that I commanded you; and lo, I am with you always, even to the end of the age. (Matt. 28:18–20)

Interestingly, the Great Commission isn't the only time Jesus "commissioned" His disciples before returning to heaven. Each

Gospel contains its own version of Jesus giving a mission to those who chose to follow Him:

- "He said to them, 'Go into all the world and preach the gospel to all creation. He who has believed and has been baptized shall be saved; but he who has disbelieved shall be condemned'" (Mark 16:15–16).

- "Then He opened their minds to understand the Scriptures, and He said to them, 'Thus it is written, that the Christ would suffer and rise again from the dead the third day, and that repentance for forgiveness of sins would be proclaimed in His name to all the nations, beginning from Jerusalem. You are witnesses of these things. And behold, I am sending forth the promise of My Father upon you; but you are to stay in the city until you are clothed with power from on high'" (Luke 24:45–49).

- "Jesus said to them again, 'Peace be with you; as the Father has sent Me, I also send you.' And when He had said this, He breathed on them and said to them, 'Receive the Holy Spirit. If you forgive the sins of any, their sins have been forgiven them; if you retain the sins of any, they have been retained'" (John 20:21–23).

Even the book of Acts contains a set of instructions from Jesus, which many people believe was part of the same conversation when He delivered the Great Commission:

It is not for you to know times or epochs which the Father has fixed by His own authority; but you will receive power when the Holy Spirit has come upon you; and you shall be My witnesses both in Jerusalem, and in all Judea and Samaria, and even to the remotest part of the earth. (Acts 1:7–8)

Taken together, those are a lot of instructions! But there's something unique about these commissions from Jesus. In each instance, they were given to the community. Each author recording these events intentionally expressed that Jesus's instructions for His followers were delivered to a community of believers rather than to an individual.

For example, in the verses from Acts 1 above, the *you* is plural. I've lived in Las Vegas for almost twenty years, but I grew up in Alabama. My friends there have an easy way to distinguish between *you* plural and *you* singular. In Alabama, *you* singular is "you." But *you* plural is "y'all." (Even as I type this, my autocorrect program fails to recognize the word *y'all*. To be honest, I'm slightly offended.)

Everywhere Jesus gave a commission to His disciples, He gave it to "y'all." Steve Moore says it this way: "The Great Commission is too big for any organization to do alone and too important for us not to try to do together."[6]

There's power in "y'all."

## Commission and Community

Let's go back to Acts 2, where church community was born. Listen to what happened in verses 46 and 47: "Day by day continuing with one mind in the temple, and breaking bread from house to house, they were taking their meals together with gladness and sincerity of heart, praising God and having favor with all the people. And the Lord was adding to their number day by day those who were being saved."

The last sentence of that verse is important: "And the Lord was adding to their number day by day those who were being saved." In the early church, these believers became connected in community, and that connection led to a shared mission. Notice that the mission was simply the overflow of community. You see, the only way we can accomplish God's global mission—which He's entrusted to us—is together. That's why God gave this commission to His church.

What do you think of when you hear the word *church*? Here's the definition, gleaned from a careful study of Scripture, we use at Hope Church: a local community of baptized Jesus followers uniting under biblical leadership to share in the mission of Christ.

According to this definition, to be a church, we must share in the mission of Christ. As we enjoy our relationship with God in fellowship with our brothers and sisters in Christ, mission automatically takes shape. If mission isn't the overflow of us enjoying our relationship with God in fellowship with others, we're not living out biblical community.

Jesus Himself forever linked our relationship with Him and our relationships with His family to His mission. Listen once again to His words in John 13:34–35: "A new commandment I give to you, that you love one another, even as I have loved you, that you also love one another. By this all men will know that you are My disciples, if you have love for one another."

According to Jesus, as the world sees our love for one another in Christian community, our love for one another becomes a testimony of our love relationship with Him. And our fellowship with one another gives evidence of our relationship with Him. That evidence is the beginning of our witness to the world. This is exactly what began happening in the book of Acts. The life of Christ in the earliest Christians was so evidenced by the love of Christ through them that the watching world was attracted to the life-changing message of the gospel. As they joined together in community, they authenticated the message of the gospel they were preaching. As a result, "the Lord was adding to their number day by day those who were being saved" (Acts 2:47).

### A Quick Evaluation

The central truth of this book is that living as a Jesus follower isn't about religion; it's about relationships. Specifically, the life of a Jesus follower revolves around three relationships that ultimately define not just what we do but who we are.

The first of those relationships is our relationship with Jesus Himself. We need to stop living *for* Jesus and instead choose to Abide in Him each day so He can live His life through us. The second is our relationship with God's family. When we abide in Christ, His power and presence overflow out of our lives and help us Connect with other Jesus followers to create a loving, supportive, encouraging community. The third relationship is our relationship with the world—with all 7.6 billion people walking the planet. And as we'll see later in this book, Jesus living His life through us won't result only in authentic, biblical community but in a genuine passion and desire to *Share* in the mission of Jesus locally and globally, taking the good news of the gospel to all who need to hear it.

That's the message of this book in a nutshell.

So before we explore the third relationship on a deeper level, let's step back and do a little critical thinking. Let's evaluate how you're currently progressing in your life as a Jesus follower. Below are some quick and easy questions to ask yourself. They correspond with each section of the Abide, Connect, Share pathway to living as a Jesus follower.

### Abide

These questions will help you examine your relationship with Jesus.

- Does my relationship with Jesus feel intimate and personal?

- Am I intentionally spending time with Jesus each day because of my love for Him and my desire to know Him better?
- Does my spiritual life have any elements of "religion" that are pushing me toward performing for God and away from knowing Him?

### Connect

These questions will help you examine your relationship with God's family.

- Am I living my life in fellowship with brothers and sisters in Christ?
- Do I regularly experience Christ working through me to provide love, support, encouragement, and even correction to other members of God's family?
- Do I allow Christ to work through other members of God's family in a way that provides love, support, encouragement, and even correction to me?

### Share

These questions will help you examine your relationship with the world.

- Am I aware of my own place in God's mission in the world?
- Have I sensed God's desire to use me in taking the good news of Jesus to my neighbors? To the nations?
- Am I ready to leverage my gifts and resources for the expansion of God's kingdom in this world?

Remember, we need to reject the pull to perform to earn God's approval. So if you're not satisfied with some of your answers to these questions, the worst thing you could do is say you're going to try harder and do more and really show everyone you're a great Jesus follower!

Instead, turn to Jesus. Spend time with Him and continue getting to know Him. As you do, He'll guide you through His plan to help you grow and mature as His disciple. And He'll overflow through your life and empower you to share in the mission of Jesus in ways you never could have imagined on your own.

# 10

## Freedom from Complacency

Everyone is called. . . . You are either a missionary or
a mission field.

J. D. Greear

Physical death is a reality in life. I know that's probably a gloomy
way to start this chapter, but nonetheless, it's true. Most of us
don't want to talk or even think about it, but we're all going to
physically die one day.

An organization established by the US Congress in 1953 called
the National Safety Council is dedicated to the promotion and
protection of life and health. Every year, the NSC releases a chart
titled "Odds of Dying." Personally, I'm captivated by this study.
That may be because I live in Las Vegas. We like to play the odds
here, so a title like that gets my attention.

Within this report are massive amounts of fascinating information. For example, it identifies heart disease as the most likely

cause of death in the United States. It reports the odds of death by this cause are 1 out of 6. I also learned that 1 out of 218,106 people in America die every year from being struck by lightning.[1] If you're like me, and odds like that are interesting to you, you'll enjoy this report.

However, one thing left me completely speechless—the odds of dying from all possible causes are 1 out of 1. Are you kidding me? An organization has been funded by Congress since 1953 just to tell us *that*?

Even though I was familiar with this annual report, I was still surprised to learn about the newest threat scientists believe is responsible for killing a large number of people every year. I've never thought of this as dangerous. It's actually something I quite enjoy: sitting.

Yes, sitting. Just getting off your feet and sitting down.

Based on recent studies, people in today's world spend more time sitting down than pretty much any other generation in human history. And it's killing us. One study claimed that "there's a direct relationship between time spent sitting and your risk of early mortality of any cause."[2] Meaning, the more time we spend sitting each day, the higher the chance we'll die an early death—and that's true regardless of age, gender, race, body mass index, and exercise habits.

According to those same studies, the best way to protect ourselves from the dangers of sitting is to get up and move. Specifically, the researchers suggested that for every thirty minutes they spend sitting down, people should spend at least five minutes walking briskly or doing some other physical activity.

From a spiritual standpoint, spending our lives in idleness as it relates to the mission of God is a harmful, deathlike blow to our joy, satisfaction, and usefulness as followers of Jesus. Specifically, for Jesus followers in America, there's a dangerous potential of limiting or even missing God's invitation to join in His work around us—and ultimately His impact through us—because we're too comfortable, too apathetic, and too unwilling to share in His mission. Far too often, if we're not intentionally pursuing Jesus, we find ourselves in a posture of spiritual complacency rather than missional urgency.

All the while, the call of God is for us to actively join in what He's doing both locally and globally.

### The Burden of Complacency

Whenever we attempt to live the Christian life in our own strength rather than live out of the overflow of our relationship with God, we face a dangerous, sinful drift to prioritizing our needs, our plans, and our comforts over the needs of those around us. That's what comes naturally to us in our own strength. Naturally, we'll swim with the current of our culture, not against it. We'll choose to serve ourselves rather than sacrifice for others. That's who we are in our own strength. But that isn't who Jesus is.

Earlier, we looked at Jesus's message to the Ephesian church in Revelation 2. Jesus criticized the Ephesians for forgetting their first love and attempting to earn spiritual favor by trying to do the right things and know the right things. If we move up to Revelation 3, we read about a church whose members had given themselves over to spiritual complacency.

Here's the message Jesus sent to the church at Laodicea:

> I know your deeds, that you are neither cold nor hot; I wish that you were cold or hot. So because you are lukewarm, and neither hot nor cold, I will spit you out of My mouth. Because you say, "I

am rich, and have become wealthy, and have need of nothing," and you do not know that you are wretched and miserable and poor and blind and naked, I advise you to buy from Me gold refined by fire so that you may become rich, and white garments so that you may clothe yourself, and that the shame of your nakedness will not be revealed; and eye salve to anoint your eyes so that you may see. (Rev. 3:15–18)

I don't know if there's anything worse than hearing Jesus Christ—our Savior and Lord—say, "I will spit you out of My mouth." And what was the reason for His disappointment with the Laodicean Christians? They were lukewarm. They embraced the gospel and received Jesus's free gift of salvation, but then they lost sight of what it meant to faithfully follow Him.

They lost sight of the mission. They became spiritually complacent.

What does a lukewarm Christian look like today? We go through the motions. We know how to say and do all the right things, and we know the bad things we're not supposed to do, but there's no yearning to be with God and leverage our lives for His mission. No passion. No life. Lukewarm Jesus followers are Christians who keep God at arm's length so they can continue doing what they like best and maintain control over their lives.

Notice that comfort is one of the root causes of this spiritual complacency. The Laodiceans were relatively wealthy. They didn't have many material needs, so they didn't feel like they needed God for much of anything. They thought they could keep their lives under control well enough by themselves.

For many Jesus followers in America, achieving the American Dream has become a good way to be comfortable and maintain the status quo. However, it's a bad foundation for our lives. It makes us lukewarm. It makes us complacent. It makes us feel like everything's okay when in reality we're spiritually naked, wretched, miserable, and blind trying to live in our own strength.

That ongoing struggle of building our comfortable, temporary empire rather than joining in the expansion of God's glorious, eternal kingdom can become a self-inflicted burden.

But there's also another burden. Too many Christians—and too many churches—operate as if salvation is the end of the spiritual journey. Too many believe the goal of "getting saved" is to go to heaven when we die. And if that's the foundation of our faith in Christ, there's not much for us to do between the moment of salvation and the day we die.

Because of these false beliefs, many Christians in our culture are "hunkering down" and attempting to enjoy life as best they can until it's time for heaven. They create bunkers within their churches—fortresses where they feel protected from the world and safe to live out their lukewarm lives until Jesus returns.

Let me tell you, I've been inside those fortresses. And they're depressing places. They're basically tombs where no spiritual life exists. Just a bunch of people waiting for the end. Just a bunch of people sitting down, wasting the precious opportunities all around them to join in the glorious mission of God.

This is also a burden of spiritual complacency.

### The Mission Is the Cure

What's the cure for the burden of spiritual complacency? Our mission! Spiritual movement.

As we saw in the previous chapter, Jesus followers have a mission to do what Jesus said: "Make disciples of all the nations, baptizing them in the name of the Father and the Son and the Holy

Spirit, teaching them to observe all that I commanded you" (Matt. 28:19–20). Jesus said to "be My witnesses both in Jerusalem, and in all Judea and Samaria, and even to the remotest part of the earth" (Acts 1:8).

Faithful Jesus followers have no time to sit around in comfortable houses being lukewarm. Nor do we have time to hunker down in spiritual fortresses. We've been sent to share in the mission of Jesus and join in the advancement of His kingdom.

In September of 2001, Hope Church held its first public worship service. Those familiar with the world of church planting would call it "Launch Sunday." From that day until now, God has been so good to us, and His invitation to my family to join in His activity of birthing this new church has been the greatest journey of my life. We've seen thousands of people come to faith in Jesus—yes, in Las Vegas. We currently have thousands of people connected in small groups and thousands gathering weekly for worship.

But early on, I had a conversation with my friend Rick Warren that caused a major shift in my thinking about the church. He said, "You measure a church's strength not by its seating capacity but by its sending capacity." He's posted that idea on social media and been widely quoted saying this as well, but as soon as I heard him say it, I wrapped my heart around it. Something about that statement resonated both within me and with whom I understood my God to be.[3]

That conversation is one of the reasons our church has, from its beginning, had a major emphasis on "sending" people out to join in God's mission. I believe God birthed our church to be a sending station for His activity both locally and globally. At Hope Church, we believe this so strongly that we emphasize sending in our membership process. In our dinner for new members, I always say, "If you join our church, we're going to do everything we can to talk you into leaving." People always laugh, but so far we've sent hundreds of our members to relocate and join in God's mission of reaching Las Vegas, the West, and the rest of the world.

Why is "sending" so important? Because being "sent" is who Jesus is.

## Sent and Light

I want to share two truths about who Jesus is and how He lives through us to fulfill His Great Commission.

The first truth is this: Jesus was sent. This is a major theme in John's Gospel. Over and over in this record of Jesus's life, John hammers the theme that Jesus didn't arrive here randomly—He was sent. Here are some examples:

- "Jesus said to them, 'My food is to do the will of Him who sent Me and to accomplish His work'" (4:34).
- "I can do nothing on My own initiative. As I hear, I judge; and My judgment is just, because I do not seek My own will, but the will of Him who sent Me" (5:30).
- "Jesus answered them and said, 'My teaching is not Mine, but His who sent Me'" (7:16).
- "He who sent Me is with Me; He has not left Me alone, for I always do the things that are pleasing to Him" (8:29).

Many similar verses are throughout the book of John, but they all point to a common question: *What mission was Jesus sent here to accomplish?* The answer is found in the second truth I want to share about Jesus: Jesus was sent to bring light.

Listen to the way Jesus describes Himself in John 12:45–46: "He who sees Me sees the One who sent Me. I have come as Light into the world, so that everyone who believes in Me will not remain in darkness."

This is Jesus talking about Himself. Notice that He says, "He who sees Me sees the One who sent Me." Jesus is saying that, when you look at Him, you see the Father who sent Him. And then He said, "I have come as Light into the world, so that everyone who believes in Me will not remain in darkness."

That's Jesus's mission. That's what He was sent here to do: to bring light.

Now, that raises another basic, yet important question: What is light? The word *light* can be defined in almost fifty different ways. For example, *light* can be defined as "not heavy." Another definition is "to ignite"; you can light wood on fire. Or if you're into equestrian sports, you might use the word *light* to describe dismounting your horse. Even if we only talked about the kind of light you can see, the English language still has more than thirty different definitions.

For example, here's one definition according to the Merriam-Webster online dictionary: "Electromagnetic radiation of any wavelength that travels in a vacuum with a speed of 299,792,458 meters (about 186,000 miles) per second."[4] Now, if this definition is the first one that popped into your mind when I asked what light is, you spend entirely too much time alone with a dictionary. Put down this book and go embrace a hobby, preferably outdoors!

My favorite definition for the word *light* is "not dark." That's a definition I can wrap my brain around. But I'd like to offer my own definition on this subject as well: light is that which makes vision possible.

The human eye is an amazing creation of God. I encourage you to Google the human eye and do some reading about its complexity. Each of our eyeballs has forty unique parts. Then some of those parts, like the retina, have more parts. For example, the retina alone has over 120 million rod and cone cells that form this one little part of the eyeball. When God made the eye, He made it so it works by taking in light and then processing that light. When all the components of the eye function properly, light is converted into electronic impulses, which are then conveyed to the brain, where an image is then perceived.

But all this complexity within the human eye doesn't work without light. There has to be a source of light for us to see anything.

For example, if you turn out all the lights in an otherwise dark room, you won't be able to see even though your eyeball is still there and all the parts are still functioning. But if you sit in the dark long enough, you *will* be able to see again. That's because we can't remove all the light from a room, and as soon as it gets dark, our eyes search for the light still there. Our pupils get smaller and larger as the amount of light goes up and down in an attempt to bring in or keep out additional light—all with the goal of enabling us to see more clearly.

If you went down into a deep cave, a place with no light at all, though, your eyes would run out of options. You could have your hand right in front of your face and not see it at all. Without light, vision isn't possible.

The same thing is true spiritually. The Bible uses this word *light* to refer to spiritual truth about God and how we can know Him. When Jesus said He came to bring light, He was saying He came to make it possible for us to know the truth about God and to come to know God personally. On our own, we would never discover the truth about God. Left to ourselves, we would never come to know God personally. God took the initiative to make Himself known to us and to reveal to us how we can know Him.

This was the mission Jesus was sent to accomplish. He came as Light to bring light. Because without *spiritual* light, it's impossible for us to see.

## His Mission Is Our Mission

The book of Hebrews opens with these words: "God, after He spoke long ago to the fathers in the prophets in many portions and in many ways . . ." (1:1). I want to focus on that phrase "long ago." The author of Hebrews was referring to what theologians call the progressive revelation of God throughout the Old Testament. That idea means God revealed Himself to His people step by step. It's almost as if God were a puzzle, and He revealed Himself one piece at a time until the world was ready to see the full picture.

For example, in creation we see the glory and power of God. Through the law, we learn of the holiness and righteousness of God. Through the prophets, we discover the patience and sovereignty of God. Through the miracles of the Old Testament and even into the New Testament, we see the authority and greatness of God. It's a progressive revelation, step by step.

According to the author of Hebrews, these were all merely glimpses. They weren't even snapshots—just pieces of the full picture. But look what happened when Jesus came: "In these last days [He] has spoken to us in His Son . . . And He is the radiance of His glory and the exact representation of His nature, and upholds all things by the word of His power" (Heb. 1:2–3).

This means that throughout the history of humanity, God has been progressively making Himself known. But when Jesus came into the world, He was the complete revelation of God. Jesus is all that God is, just with skin on. Have you ever been asked by a little child, "What's God like?" The answer is easy: "Jesus." The Bible teaches that God had progressively made Himself known, starting with creation, but in Jesus we have the exact representation of God's nature. We have Him in the flesh. That's why Paul said, "In [Jesus] all the fullness of Deity dwells in bodily form" (Col. 2:9).

Jesus once and for all fully revealed the truth about God and how we could know Him personally. That's why, as we look back at His words from earlier in this chapter—"He who sees Me sees the One who sent Me" (John 12:45)—we understand Him to say, "When you see Me you've seen God. All that God is, I am." Jesus said about Himself, "When you see Me you see the One who sent Me. I've come as Light into the world." Why? "So that everyone who believes in Me will not remain in darkness" (John 12:46).

Through Jesus, the people of the earth have the ability to know the truth about God and to know Him personally. Jesus was sent on a mission for that to happen.

You may be thinking, *That's great. But that's Jesus's mission. What does that have to do with me?* I'm so glad you asked. If you catch the truth I'm about to share with you from the words of Jesus, your perspective about your life will never be the same. Let's look at two verses that are absolutely critical to understanding our mission.

The first verse is in the most intimate conversation between Jesus and His Father recorded anywhere in the New Testament. John 17 is a recorded prayer between Jesus and the Father, and it's incredible in so many ways. But look specifically at verse 18, where Jesus says, "As You sent Me into the world, I also have sent them into the world."

Let that sink in. Jesus looked at the Father and said, "Father, as You have sent Me into the world, I also have sent them."

Well, who was *them*? A couple sentences later, Jesus identifies *them* as "those also who believe in Me through their word" (v. 20). That means "them" was Jesus's immediate disciples—and everyone who would become a follower of Jesus through their witness. So Jesus was referring to every Christian in every generation when He said, "As You sent Me into the world, I also have sent them."

That includes you and me.

In the second verse I want to explore, Jesus is also challenging His disciples, this time in John's version of the Great Commission. In John 20:21, Jesus says to them, "As the Father has sent Me, I also send you." Are you getting the picture? Is the Holy Spirit of God revealing this truth to you?

We have the same mission Jesus did! We're sent to the same place with the same purpose.

If you're still not clear on this truth, look at what Jesus said in Matthew 5:14: "You are the light of the world." *What? Wait a minute! I thought Jesus said He was the Light of the world in the book of John.* Well, He is. But we are too. Now Jesus operates as the Light of the world *through* us. Again, that tells us all we need to know about our mission. You and I have been sent into the world, so through Christ in us, our neighbors and the nations may know the truth about God and come to know Him personally.

How could we possibly experience spiritual complacency and apathy if we've embraced such a mission? We can't. It's not possible for us to remain lukewarm if we're truly experiencing the Light of the world bursting through our lives and piercing the darkness of the world.

So ask yourself if that's what you've been experiencing in your spiritual walk. Are you an active part of Jesus's mission?

### The Aroma of Life

Of all the authors in the New Testament, no one wrote more about the power of Christ's life being lived out through us than the apostle Paul. In his second letter to the church in Corinth, he writes these words that powerfully express the idea of Christ living through us on mission:

> Thanks be to God, who always leads us in triumph in Christ, and manifests through us the sweet aroma of the knowledge of Him in every place. For we are a fragrance of Christ to God among those who are being saved and among those who are perishing; to the one an aroma from death to death, to the other an aroma from life to life. And who is adequate for these things? For we are not like many, peddling the word of God, but as from sincerity, but as from God, we speak in Christ in the sight of God. (2 Cor. 2:14–17)

This is an incredible vision for Jesus followers everywhere—that we can serve as "an aroma from life to life" for those who need to experience the truth of the gospel.

Although Paul makes it clear that our involvement in God's mission is totally a work of God, he also makes it clear that it's a work God is doing through us. Meaning, God does the work of creating this sweet aroma, but it's experienced by others out of the overflow of our pursuit of Him.

Now, here's an interesting thing to notice. Paul said in verse 15, "For we are a fragrance of Christ to God." Wait a minute. Shouldn't that say, "We are a fragrance of Christ to *them*"? Meaning the world? Isn't the whole point that Christ in us will accomplish His mission in the people around us?

Let me give you a life-changing perspective. The focus is not *them*; the focus is *Him*. But as we focus on *Him*, He makes Himself known to *them* through our lives. Here's the way Clyde Cranford writes about this passage from 2 Corinthians: "If we are walking in intimacy with Christ, the sweet smell of His presence in our lives rises first to the nostrils of God as a fragrant aroma. Then this fragrance disseminates to those around us."[5]

The word *manifest* from verse 14 comes from a Greek word that means to make visible, to show openly, or to make known. Here, then, is the principle: as God transforms our lives through our relationship with Him, Christ in us is made visible through our lives. This means "living sent" isn't about doing evangelism and mission as much as it's about being conformed to the image of Christ as the overflow of my relationship with the Father. Sharing in the mission isn't really a mission issue in my life; sharing in the mission is an issue of Christlikeness. Sharing in the mission is the life of Jesus made visible through my life. Meaning, if I struggle in the areas of evangelism and joining in God's global activity, that doesn't mean I need to grow in the area of "mission." That reveals a lack of Christlikeness in me that can be changed only through a deeper pursuit of intimate fellowship with God. "Mission" is what God does out of the overflow of my relationship with Him.

What if these truths became a reality? What if the sweet aroma of the knowledge of Jesus was made known everywhere your foot hit the ground this week? What if that were true in the life of every Jesus follower in the world? Every school, every job, every neighborhood, every apartment complex, every grocery store, every mall would be filled with "the sweet aroma of the knowledge of Him" (2 Cor. 2:14).

That, my friend, would change the world!

Here's a reality we need to keep in mind as we think through how Christ accomplishes His mission through us: God does it. Look back at how Paul begins verse 14: "Thanks be to God." He didn't say thanks be to you, the Christians. He didn't say thanks be to you, the church. He didn't say thanks be to the preachers or missionaries or evangelists. No. Paul said thanks be to God. Thanks be to God, who leads. Thanks be to God, who manifests.

As Paul reminds us here, it's not about us. It's thanks be to God, not to us. When we see God's mission advance, it's only because of God manifesting the life of Christ in and through us. Paul is reminding us that the Christian life isn't about us doing something for Jesus; the Christian life is about us being with Jesus and then allowing Him to work through us to accomplish His mission.

That's why a little later on in this letter to the church at Corinth, Paul said, "Not that we are adequate in ourselves to consider anything as coming from ourselves, but our adequacy is from God" (2 Cor. 3:5). If your life or mine has any eternal effect on the mission of God, it's not because of anything we've done. It's because of everything Jesus has done in and through us.

Think back to our three key words—*Abide*, *Connect*, and *Share*. When I'm living in an abiding, intimate, personal relationship with God that's allowing me to connect in fellowship with my brothers and sisters in Christ, my relationship with God will be challenged, will grow, and will expand. Out of the overflow of this, Jesus spills out. Christ in us, living through us.

This is the point: if we're genuinely abiding and connecting, sharing just happens. If there's no sharing in the mission, there's also an issue with abiding and connecting.

Remember my friend Drew from the previous chapter? My life opened the door for me to speak the good news of Jesus to him, but only because Christ had been spilling out through me. For over a year, Drew had watched my life. He smelled the sweet aroma of Christ and longed for Him.

But I get it wrong a lot too. Recently I was at Costco, just trying to get my new card and out the door. If you go there on a Saturday, it's a crazy zoo. Yet here I am in the midst of the madness, standing in line, and the guy behind me just wants to talk. And talk. And talk. In my mind, I'm screaming, *I don't want to talk! I want to get my card and leave!* I do everything I can to cut him off, but this guy really wants to have a conversation with me. Finally, I reach the front of the line and get my card. Then I turn and almost run out the door.

As I was driving to my church office the next day, the Holy Spirit clearly brought that man's face to my mind. And in my spirit, I heard that still, small voice whisper, *Vance, what happened yesterday? I want to use you in every place.* I was reminded again that we're always on mission. Every one of us has moments like that every day. Sometimes we get it right; sometimes we get it wrong.

With Drew, by God's grace and the power of Christ in me, I got it right. In Costco, in my own flesh and strength, I got it wrong. And God pierced my heart about it. He wanted that guy in Costco to know He loves him. God sent me to Costco to tell him.

Some Christians say the world is hostile to the gospel. They argue that people don't want to hear the good news about Jesus. I don't think that's true. I think they just want to know that what we're preaching about Jesus is real. The big question is whether what you and I are inviting them to on Sunday makes any difference in our lives on Monday.

In his book titled *The Church of Irresistible Influence*, Robert Lewis writes this:

> The world is tired of the church impersonally talking it down and chewing it up. What the world waits to see is whether what we have is better than what they have. Just think what bridges we could build if we truly followed the example of the New Testament church. We would go beyond being seeker-sensitive, to a new frontier of being community-admired. We would be known, not just

by the corner we inhabit, but by the city with which we interact. And people would be drawn to God, not because of the weekly show in our churches, but by the irrefutable lives we incarnate.[6]

What if people showed up at your church on Sunday and said, "You know what? I don't know anything about your church, but I know some of the people who go here. I don't know what they have, but I want it because I've seen it in their lives." That's the goal. Really, that's how it should work—if Christ is spilling out of our lives in that sweet aroma.

## Be Sincere

As we close this chapter, it's important to note that God also accomplishes His mission through our lips. Our lives authenticate the message of the gospel, but the message of the gospel must still be shared verbally. Paul writes about sharing the gospel in 2 Corinthians 2:17, saying, "We speak in Christ."

Our lives are important, but the Christian life isn't just about living an authentic lifestyle. Sometimes we're to open our mouths and share the good news. Faith comes by hearing. People need to hear the message of Christ. Therefore, we need to be equipped to share the gospel. Every one of us should be able to share our personal story of coming to Christ.

In verse 17, Paul also emphasized that we should speak "as from sincerity." The word *sincerity* comes from an interesting Greek word, commonly used by craftsmen in the art of pottery. When making a new piece, the potter molded it into the desired shape and then put it into an oven. But an inexperienced potter might make the oven too hot or leave the pot in too long, causing the pot to crack. An honest potter would throw away the piece and start over. A dishonest potter would fill the cracks with wax and then conceal them with paint.

The average buyer in the market would purchase the pot, take it home, and never know the difference—until the pot leaked. But a skilled buyer would hold the pot up to the light of the sun, turning it slowly to discover any hidden cracks. After determining the pot had no cracks, that buyer would say, "This pot is sincere."

So Paul was teaching us that the world is holding up our lives and looking at them—every day. People want to know if the way we live is consistent with what we're saying. They want to know if we're sincere.

That's an important question. Are you sincere? Every day, where you live, work, and play, are you genuinely allowing Christ in you, out of the overflow of your relationship with the Father, to accomplish His mission? Remember, your mission is the same as Christ's mission. You are the plan. Almost eight billion people live on planet Earth. And as you focus on Jesus, He will accomplish His mission by making Himself known to them through you.

As those moments turn into a lifestyle, you will be forever removed from spiritual sitting. You will be forever free from the burden of complacency.

# 11

## Freedom from This World

My biggest fear, even now, is that I will hear Jesus'
words and walk away, content to settle for less than
radical obedience to him.

David Platt

Just a few days ago, I read a statistic that stopped me in my tracks:
more than 50 percent of churchgoers are unfamiliar with the Great
Commission. More than 50 percent! I had a hard time believing
that could be true, so I dug a little deeper. The study making this
claim was put together by the Barna Group and the Seed Project—
reputable sources. And the question on the survey was simply this:
"Have you heard of the Great Commission?"

Here's how the churchgoers answered:

- "Yes, and I know what it means"—17 percent.
- "Yes, but I can't recall the exact meaning"—25 percent.

- "No"—51 percent.
- "I'm not sure"—6 percent.

Another section of the study listed several passages of Scripture—including Matthew 28:18–20, which contains the Great Commission—and asked participants to pick the correct passage from that list. This time, only 37 percent of churchgoers chose the correct passage.[1]

These are shocking numbers. If people in our churches have never heard of the Great Commission, they certainly aren't carrying out the Great Commission. They're missing out on their God-given opportunity to *Share* in the mission of Jesus, taking the good news of the gospel to the peoples of the earth.

That's a tragedy. And one of the reasons for that tragedy is that too many Jesus followers are far too comfortable living as part of the world.

### The Burden of the World

We've explored a couple of the messages Jesus delivered to specific churches in the region of Asia Minor through the apostle John. Here's the message Jesus sent to the church at Sardis:

> I know your deeds, that you have a name that you are alive, but you are dead. Wake up, and strengthen the things that remain, which were about to die; for I have not found your deeds completed in the sight of My God. So remember what you have received and heard; and keep it, and repent. Therefore if you do not wake up, I will come like a thief, and you will not know at what hour I will come to you. (Rev. 3:1–3)

Ouch! Remember, this was written to a congregation of Christians. And what was Jesus's critique? They were spiritually dead.

They gave no evidence of the transformation and new life they claimed to have experienced as Jesus followers. In other words, there was little or no difference between the Christians in Sardis and the non-Christians in Sardis. They had become just like the world around them.

In the previous chapter, we explored how some Jesus followers fail to share in God's mission because they turn their churches into spiritual bunkers and retreat from the rest of the world. This is a problem, because our mission as Jesus followers is to make disciples in the world. Therefore, hiding from the world leads to spiritual stagnation and a lack of purpose, which can become heavy burdens.

In this passage, the Christians of Sardis had gone in the opposite direction. They had assimilated themselves into the world to such a degree that they were no longer different from the world. They had lost their spiritual life—their spiritual vitality. This is also an incredible burden, because the world is opposed to Christ.

Remember what Jesus said in Matthew 6:24? "No one can serve two masters; for either he will hate the one and love the other, or he will be devoted to one and despise the other. You cannot serve God and wealth." Yes, Jesus was talking specifically about money in that passage, but the principle carries through when we try to place anything on an equal level with God.

Let me tell you something from experience; trying to serve two masters is a heavy burden. I understand the pull of wanting to be like everyone else. I understand the fascination that can develop with the things of this world—the comfort and the luxury and the status and everything that seems like it will be so much fun.

But I also know this: we create a terrible weight around our shoulders when we try to follow both Jesus and the world.

And here's something else I know: the antidote to the burden of being pulled too far *into* the world is feeling the purpose and satisfaction of joining God's mission *for* the world as a functioning citizen of His kingdom.

### The Kingdom of God

Earlier, I shared that my life drastically changed over a two-year period when I had the privilege of being mentored by Clyde Cranford. One of the ways Clyde helped me was by constantly pointing me back to the Scriptures, encouraging me to immerse myself in God's Word.

One September morning in 1999, I was beginning to work my way through the Gospel of Luke. As I finished reading through chapter 4, I had an experience that forever changed the course of my life. Here's what I read:

> When day came, Jesus left and went to a secluded place; and the crowds were searching for Him, and came to Him and tried to keep Him from going away from them. But He said to them, "I must preach the kingdom of God to the other cities also, for I was sent for this purpose."
>
> So he kept on preaching in the synagogues of Judea. (vv. 42–44)

If you've been walking with God for some time, you know the difference between reading the Bible and God speaking from His Word. On that particular morning, God was speaking to me through His Word. I didn't hear an audible voice, but it was as if the Holy Spirit pulled me into that passage of Scripture and poured truth about Jesus into my life.

And here's a principle that jumped off the page for me: *As I follow Jesus, what is on His heart will be on my heart.*

This only makes sense, right? This principle happens in any relationship. If you spend enough time with someone, you start caring about what they care about. For example, when I was in college, I wore absolutely every piece of clothing I owned before I did laundry. Only when everything was dirty—and I mean everything—was it finally time to wash my clothes. But sometimes I first recycled lightly worn clothing if it could pass the smell test. I didn't care much about clean.

Fast-forward to today. I have now been married for almost three decades, and I've spent much of that time with my wife. Kristie is passionate about clean. And when I say passionate, I mean *passionate*. In our home, we have two categories for clean: "clean" and "Kristie clean."

So after all this time with my wife, do you know what I've found? I now care about things being clean. Not only that, but I care about several other things I never used to care about—all because of how much time I've spent with her. As our relationship developed, what was on her heart began to have a place on my heart.

The same thing happens in your relationship with Jesus. As you walk with Him, what is on His heart begins to be on your heart. So when I read Luke 4 that morning, I started to see what was on the heart of Jesus more clearly.

Here's what Jesus said in Luke 4:43 that struck me: "I must preach the kingdom of God." We can become so familiar with the stories of the Bible that we read right over the emotion and passion of the words. This was no casual statement Jesus was making. And the way it's constructed in the Greek language, it describes a consuming passion—His passion—every minute of every hour, every hour of every day, every day of every week, every week of every month, and every month of every year.

As I sat there overwhelmed by the passion of Jesus, I grew deeply convicted that the passion I saw in Him was not in me. I was Jesus's disciple, but I wasn't passionate about the same thing He was. And I didn't share anything close to His level of passion.

In that moment, my heart was broken. I realized I was focused more on the things of this world than on the expansion of God's kingdom. This was an encumbrance weighing me down, and I had no idea until the Holy Spirit spoke to me through His Word.

Jesus was passionate about God's kingdom. Did you hear His declaration? He said, "I *must* preach the kingdom of God." Before I read in Luke's Gospel that morning, I had asked the Holy Spirit to show me a truth about Jesus that was not a truth in me. Then this word *must* leapt off the page. I suddenly noticed this consuming passion of Jesus for the kingdom of God. And if I'm going to be completely honest with you, I have to admit that not only was I not passionate about the kingdom of God but I didn't even know what the kingdom of God was all about. And yet here was Jesus, crying out that the consuming passion of His life every moment of every day was the kingdom of God.

So I set out on a journey to explore the kingdom of God, to figure it out.

## What Is the Kingdom?

Did you know that over one hundred references to the "kingdom of God" are spread across sixteen different books of the New Testament? Obviously, it's an important theme. But what is the kingdom of God?

Here's my definition after almost two decades of study: the kingdom of God is God's sovereign activity in the world resulting in people being in right relationship with Himself.

The kingdom of God is the big picture of what God is doing in the world, the global mission of God. God in His sovereignty is at work in the world, and as a result of His activity, people are being born again into a right relationship with Him.

Here are some other truths I've learned about the kingdom of God that will help us understand our part as we faithfully share in God's mission:

- *The kingdom is believers.* Whenever you meet someone who's been born again through the shed blood of Jesus Christ on the cross, you meet an expression of the kingdom of God. If you're a follower of Jesus Christ, you're a visible expression of the kingdom of God. That means you and I aren't simply members of a church; we're citizens of a kingdom. And it's a glorious kingdom that's alive and expanding all over the world. The kingdom of God is believers.

- *The kingdom is big.* In Revelation 5:9, the kingdom of God is described as "every tribe and tongue and people and nation." That's significant, because what we read in Revelation is the real end of the story. It's the glorious, grand climax of the eternal, redemptive mission of God. It will be huge, and it will involve the incredible expanse of God's kingdom.

- *The kingdom is being built.* Matthew 24:14 says, "This gospel of the kingdom shall be preached in the whole world as a testimony to all the nations, and then the end will come." The end of what? The end of the world as we know it. We've become so comfortable with our "make me feel better and meet my needs" brand of Christianity in North America that we've forgotten the mission of God is moving toward a glorious ending. One day King Jesus will step out of eternity and into our world, bringing time as we know it to an end. The Bible describes that moment in 1 Thessalonians 4:16–17:

> The Lord Himself will descend from heaven with a shout, with the voice of the archangel and with the trumpet of God, and the dead in Christ will rise first. Then we who are alive and remain will be caught up together with them in the clouds to meet the Lord in the air, and so we shall always be with the Lord.

God in His sovereignty is at work all over the world, establishing His kingdom. His kingdom is believers. His kingdom is big. His kingdom is being built. And God didn't bring you to Himself just to bless your life and give you your best life now. God brought you to Himself so out of the overflow of your intimate love relationship with Him—which is Christ in you, working through you— you could share in His mission locally and globally in fellowship with others.

What we learn from Christ's life in Luke 4 is that this is exactly who Jesus is. Jesus shared in the mission of the Father out of the overflow of His intimate love relationship with Him. In the same way, to the degree that you are allowing Christ *in* you to live *through* you, you will share in the mission of the kingdom. This means mission is not what you do as a follower of Jesus; as a Jesus follower, all of life is now lived on mission.

The scene we read in Revelation 5 is a moment already established in eternity. It's done. It's not describing a potential outcome or what might happen in the future. It's describing a future already established in eternity. The question for you and me today is whether we will be a part of what God is doing in establishing His kingdom.

Jesus said about the kingdom of God, "I must!" Is that the cry of your heart today? Do you have a passion for God's kingdom to be expanded? Are you passionate about the gospel engaging the lives of people in your city? Are the peoples of the earth on your heart? Are you leveraging your life for the sake of God's kingdom?

Or are you being dragged down by living like the rest of the world?

## The Greatest Obstacle to God's Kingdom

As Jesus followers, we have an enemy. Simon Peter, one of Jesus's first followers, knew about the reality of this enemy all too well. In Luke 22:31–32, Jesus said, "Simon, Simon, behold, Satan has demanded permission to sift you like wheat; but I have prayed for you, that your faith may not fail; and you, when once you have turned again, strengthen your brothers."

Because Peter knew the reality of struggling against the onslaught of our enemy personally, he reminded us to "be of sober spirit, be on the alert. Your adversary, the devil, prowls around like a roaring lion, seeking someone to devour" (1 Pet. 5:8). If you become passionate about God's kingdom being expanded, and if you leverage your life for the sake of the kingdom, the enemy will take notice and oppose you.

Doing church "as usual" doesn't offend Satan. Going through the motions of church and simply practicing religion are weapons he uses to lure people away from a real relationship with God. When it comes to the expansion of God's kingdom, he has many weapons he attempts to use as obstacles.

Here's an interesting question: What do you think is the greatest obstacle to the expansion of God's kingdom in the world?

Some would argue that the greatest obstacle today is the persecution of believers. From the Middle East throughout South Asia, China, and all the way to Central America, followers of Jesus suffer at the hands of vicious persecutors all over the world. According to Open Doors USA, in the last year, over 245 million Christians were living in places where they experience high levels of persecution; 4,305 Christians were killed for their faith, 1,847 churches and other Christian buildings were attacked; and 3,150 Christians were detained without trial, arrested, sentenced, or imprisoned.[2] This is nothing new. It's the same persecution our brothers and sisters in Christ faced in the first century. It's why Peter warned them to "not be surprised at the fiery ordeal among you" (1 Pet. 4:12), and neither should we.

If the enemy had his way, he would use persecution to stamp out the kingdom of God. But as you study places where the church is persecuted, you'll find they're some of the strongest growth areas of Christianity in the world. Tertullian, an early church father, even said, "The blood of the martyrs is the seed of the church."[3] Since the stoning of Stephen, the expansion of God's kingdom has always come from believers willing to give their lives for the sake of the gospel.

As an example, Iran is one of the ten countries where it's most dangerous to follow Jesus. And yet, according to workers in the field, six hundred people are coming to faith in Jesus Christ every month there. They testify that more people have come to Christ in Iran in the last one hundred years than in the previous nineteen centuries combined.[4]

So persecution isn't the greatest obstacle to the expansion of God's kingdom in the world.

Others argue that the greatest obstacle to the expansion of God's kingdom in the world today is false teaching. They say our enemy's ability to twist and distort truth is his greatest weapon against us.

Certainly, false teaching is dangerous for the church. Jesus warned against it in Matthew 7, saying, "Beware of the false prophets, who come to you in sheep's clothing, but inwardly are ravenous wolves. You will know them by their fruits. Grapes are not gathered from thorn bushes nor figs from thistles, are they? So every good tree bears good fruit, but the bad tree bears bad fruit" (vv. 15–17). However, because Jesus followers have the Word of God at their disposal to test the message of any new teaching, we have an effective shield against false teachers and prophets. (This is another reason we must not forget that some people groups still don't have the Word translated into their own language.)

As we look back to Luke 4:42–44, we learn that the greatest obstacle to the expansion of God's kingdom in the world is not persecution and it's not false teaching or even our enemy. Read these verses again and see if you can identify the great obstacle to God's mission in the world:

> When day came, Jesus left and went to a secluded place; and the crowds were searching for Him, and came to Him and tried to keep Him from going away from them. But He said to them, "I must preach the kingdom of God to the other cities also, for I was sent for this purpose."
> So He kept on preaching in the synagogue of Judea.

In Luke 4, we see Jesus living out a full day of ministry. The people heard Him preach. Verse 32 says, "They were amazed at His teaching, for His message was with authority." The people had never heard anyone teach and preach like Jesus did.

The people in Luke 4 witnessed the supernatural power of Jesus. In verses 35–38, He displayed this power as He cast out demons.

As a result, "amazement came upon them all. . . . And the report about Him was spreading into every locality in the surrounding district." The people were in awe of the power of Jesus.

They also experienced the compassion of Jesus. In verses 38–41, the people were bringing to Him all those with various diseases. The Bible says He was "laying His hands on each one of them" and He healed them. This is one of the few places in Scripture I recall Jesus healing every person who was present and in need of healing. His compassion overwhelmed the people as He laid hands on every afflicted one.

So in that one incredible day of ministry, the people heard Jesus's preaching and were amazed. They saw His power and were astonished. They experienced His compassion and were overwhelmed. But then in verse 42, Luke says, they "tried to keep Him from going away from them." After experiencing the amazing life of Jesus, here was the people's response: let us keep this all to ourselves!

Do you see the greatest obstacle to the expansion of God's kingdom? The self-centeredness of the people of God. The people in Luke 4 cared more about themselves and their needs than they cared about the world Jesus came to save. But before we become too critical of them, we must realize that we often have exactly the same response. We've been saved by the grace of Jesus. We've experienced the life of Jesus. We've been blessed by the provision of Jesus. We've received encouragement from the family of Jesus. But too often our attitude is just like the one people in this story had: let's just keep this all to ourselves.

It's impossible for you to truthfully say, "My relationship with God is good," if you don't have a passion for His kingdom to be expanded locally and globally. You're lying to yourself if you think your relationship with God is good but you're not engaging His mission to expand His kingdom to the ends of the earth, beginning right where you live.

Unfortunately, we've created a Christianity that says, "Mission is for the super Christian." Or "Mission is something most of us just give some money toward." Or "Mission is for someone else to do while we pray." But as we examine the life of Christ in the Gospels, we learn that mission is who Jesus is. As a result, to the degree we're conformed to the image of Christ, we see our lives, our families, our jobs, our careers, our skills, our hobbies, and even our retirements as being on mission—to be used by God to expand His kingdom for His glory.

So let me ask you a question. Is the consuming passion of your life to build your empire? Or is it to expand God's kingdom?

My good friend David Platt wrote a book titled *Radical* that drills deep into this question. Here's what he says:

> We were settling for a Christianity that revolves around catering to ourselves when the central message of Christianity is actually about abandoning ourselves. . . . We will not wish we had made more money, acquired more stuff, lived more comfortably, taken more vacations, watched more television, pursued greater retirement, or been more successful in the eyes of this world. Instead we will wish we had given more of ourselves to living for the day when every nation, tribe, people, and language will bow around the throne and sing the praises of the Savior who delights in radical obedience and the God who deserves eternal worship.[5]

We have developed so many excuses for not joining in God's mission. We say, "Well, when I get my career established, then I'll . . ." Or "When I get my portfolio just right, then I'll . . ." Or "When I get through this season of life, and I get my kids raised, then I'll . . ." Hear me. There's nothing wrong with career advancement, portfolios, or raising a family, but we should see all those things leveraged for the expansion of God's kingdom every day where we live, work, and play. Our whole lives have been brought into relationship with God to live on mission with Him.

### Fellowship with the Father

How did Jesus overcome this obstacle of selfishness among His followers? Luke 4:42 opens with "When day came, Jesus left and went to a secluded place." Now, Luke doesn't tell us what Jesus did there, but Mark does in his account of this same event. Mark 1:35 says, "In the early morning, while it was still dark, Jesus got up, left the house, and went away to a secluded place, and was praying there."

Jesus maintained the heart of the Father by spending intimate moments alone with Him in fellowship. And out of the overflow of that fellowship, He kept a firm hold on His mission to reach not just a community or a church but the world.

Listen, I get it. Every day we have to fight the temptation to live our lives in pursuit of our dreams. In *Radical*, Platt notes that "we desperately need to explore how much of our understanding of the gospel is American and how much is biblical."[6] How do I ensure that my dreams don't become the consuming passion of my life? How do I seek first the kingdom of God? Do I make more commitments to be involved in mission and evangelism? That's not the answer. The answer is in following the example of Jesus. We must be with the Father.

Here's a second major truth from Luke 4 that radically changed my life: *my relationship to the world is dependent on my fellowship with the Father.*

In those moments when human selfishness threatens to derail my mission—whether it's my own selfishness or that of others—I must follow the example of Jesus and pull away to be with God. And as I'm with Him, He warms my heart again for those things on His heart. My fellowship with the Father is what allows me to maintain a right relationship with the world.

To be honest, left to myself and my own flesh, I don't care about others as much as I care about myself. And if you'll be honest, you'll say the same about yourself. But Christ in us allows us to see people the way He sees them. And the more we see people the way He sees them, the more that changes how we live.

That leads me to the final truth from Luke 4 that changed my life: *the life I live should reflect the purpose I have.*

I love the way Luke ends this story. In verse 44, he says, "So He kept on preaching." The people said to Jesus, "Stay here, Lord!" But Jesus said, "I'm about something bigger. I'm about my Father's kingdom business." So He went from city to city and place to place and continued to join in the expansion of God's kingdom. You see, the life He lived reflected the purpose He had.

### Say Yes

Let me take you back to that September morning in 1999. I'm in Memphis, Tennessee, and I'm alone with the Father. I'm pursuing Christ's life in the Gospel of Luke, and I finally understand the three truths I've shared with you in this chapter. In that moment, God absolutely breaks me. What the Holy Spirit had so lovingly and yet firmly revealed to me about the life of Jesus isn't present in my life.

I ask my wife to join me in the living room, and then I share with her what I've just shared with you from Luke 4. Then we kneel, and we cry out to God, "Lord, yes."

You may ask what question we were answering. We didn't know. We just knew the answer needed to be yes. We said yes to whenever, wherever, whatever, and however God chose to use our family and our future to expand His kingdom for His glory.

Two weeks later, a pastor named Johnny Hunt, who had greatly influenced my life, approached me. He said, "Vance, our church feels led of the Lord to start a new church in Las Vegas, Nevada. God has put it on my heart that we are to send you and your family to plant it."

The rest of the story is that my family, along with many others, have spent the last two decades joining in God's kingdom activity in the city of Las Vegas, attempting to live out Luke 4. The passion of Hope Church is "I must." We are a fellowship of people deeply in love with Jesus, enjoying fellowship with one another, and living with our "yes" on the table to join in the expansion of God's kingdom.

To be honest, when my wife and I knelt in Memphis and said, "Lord, yes," we were somewhat afraid of the journey God would take us on as a family. You see, we had young children and what we thought was a pretty good plan for our future. But I can say with absolute certainty that the last two decades have been the most incredible ride of my life. I have truly learned that the joy is in the journey.

Is your yes on the table? That's a scary question to answer. His invitation might be to leverage your job, or where you live, for His glory and the expansion of His kingdom, but He might send you to the other side of the world.

Here's what I can promise you, though: as you Abide in Christ, Connect in community, and Share in the mission, you'll enjoy all the life God has in store for you.

# 12

# The 5 Percent Life Challenge

The resources of the Christian life, my friends, are just—Jesus Christ. . . . The many references throughout the New Testament to Christ in you, and you in Christ, Christ our life, and abiding in Christ, are literal, actual, blessed fact, and not figures of speech. . . . Jesus Christ does not want to be our helper; He wants to be our life. He does not want us to work for Him. He wants us to let Him do His work through us, using us as we use a pencil to write with—better still, using us as one of the fingers on His hand.

Charles Trumbull

I grew up in the 1970s, smack in the middle of the Cold War between the United States and the Soviet Union. It was a tense time, to say the least. Everyone lived in fear of nuclear war, but you still had to go about your day. I remember the drills at school. We had to practice getting under our desks in case of an attack—although I never did figure out how that desk was supposed to protect me from anything more dangerous than a spitball.

In any case, as part of its defense plan, the United States invested billions of dollars to develop a global positioning system for submarines. The goal was to improve navigation for our subs but also to obtain an accurate fix on the positions of Russian subs prior to launching ballistic missiles.

Back in the 1980s, you would have been hard-pressed to find anyone who thought any real good could come from something so serious. But it did! In 1983, President Ronald Reagan announced that the global positioning system was being made available for civilian use. Today we call it GPS. And because of that amazing technology, all you have to do to get turn-by-turn directions to the nearest Chick-fil-A whenever you get a craving for a chicken sandwich is type "Chick-fil-A" into your smartphone.

Now, I really do think GPS technology is amazing, and I use it all the time. But sometimes I feel like I just need to go out on my own. Maybe it's a man thing. Maybe it's a lingering form of pride. I don't know. But it's there.

One of those times occurred not long ago when I was traveling out of state with my good friend Travis Ogle, the senior executive pastor at our church. The two of us had eaten at a nice restaurant the previous evening, and we thought it was a good idea to eat there again. So we hopped into the car and hit the road without using GPS. We didn't need directions to find a place we'd just been to the day before, right?

After about ten minutes, we realized we were passing stores and malls we hadn't noticed before, and the names of the cross streets weren't familiar either. Not wanting to be stubborn about it, I went ahead and typed the name of the restaurant into the GPS app on my phone. Sure enough, the first thing the computerized voice said was, "As soon as possible, make a legal U-turn."

We were going in the completely wrong direction. The lesson I learned from that experience is that it's easy to get lost when we put too much confidence in our own strength and our own ability to figure things out.

I think the same is true in our spiritual lives. We do much better when we have directions to follow. And at Hope Church, we call that the 5 Percent Life Challenge.

## It's about Time

Throughout our journey together in this book, we've sought to answer the question, *What does it look like to faithfully follow Jesus?* My prayer is that the paradigm we've established with these three relationships—our relationship with God, our relationship with God's family (the church), and our relationship with the world—has brought you clarity in answering that question.

But I'd like to address another question that's probably on your mind: *If following Jesus is all about the three relationships of abiding in Christ, connecting in community, and sharing in the mission, how do I develop these relationships and grow as a follower of Jesus?*

You see, it's one thing to say, "I get it! Following Jesus is all about relationships—a relationship with God spills into my relationships with God's family and then overflows into relationships with people who don't know God to join in the mission of God. I really get it!" But if all that's true, what's the plan to make it work in your life?

The answer is simple. We deepen those relationships the same way we deepen any relationship—through *time*.

Here's a final principle to keep in mind: *every relationship in my life is developed by choosing to invest time in that relationship.*

The only way to deepen and grow any relationship is by choosing to invest your time in it. When Kristie and I choose to spend time alone by going on a date or getting away for the weekend, that's personal, one-on-one time with her. But that one-on-one time with her affects all the other relationships in my family. That's because my relationship with my wife is the foundation of our family. As my relationship with her improves, all the other relationships in my family improve.

I also spend one-on-one time with each of my children. Or sometimes we all choose to spend time together over a meal or on a trip. Some of my favorite times now are the special moments I get to spend one-on-one with my granddaughter. The bottom line is that I choose many different ways to invest my time and deepen each of these unique relationships.

In the same way, if you and I want to deepen the three relationships that establish the paradigm for faithfully following Jesus—Abide, Connect, and Share—we must choose to invest time in them.

**Four Ways to Invest Our Time**

I believe that to grow all three of these relationships as a Jesus follower, you must invest your time in four strategic ways. All four of these strategic ways are present in the life of Jesus in the Gospels, practiced in the early church as recorded in the Scriptures, and evident in church history throughout the centuries.

The first investment is what I call *God Time*. This is time spent alone in fellowship with God daily. Jesus modeled this for us by prioritizing time alone with the Father in His own life. Disciples in the early church were recognized by others as men and women who had been with Jesus. In the same way, it's imperative that you choose to set aside time to be alone with Jesus daily. Everything in your life will rise and fall based on your time alone with Him.

As Clyde Cranford writes,

> For the Christian, his entire life is to be an intimate walk with God. But that intimacy is developed one day at a time as he sets aside, each day, some increment of time exclusively for communion with his God. . . . There is no substitute for this time. This is where intimacy begins.[1]

The second strategic way you must choose to invest your time is what I call *Gather Time*. This is time gathering with your church in worship weekly. Again, we see this modeled in the life of Christ. Before His death, burial, and resurrection, it was Jesus's custom to gather with God's people in the synagogue on the Sabbath day for worship. This Sabbath practice then became the Sunday pattern of the early church after the resurrection.

A Christian apologist in the second century named Justin Martyr describes the early church in his writings this way:

> And on the day called Sunday, all who live in cities or in the country gather together to one place, and the memoirs of the apostles or the writings of the prophets are read, as long as time permits; then, when the reader has ceased, the president verbally instructs, and exhorts to the imitation of these good things. Then we all rise together and pray.[2]

When we gather for worship, we're not following some American version of Christianity. We're following in the footsteps of Jesus and those in the early church by giving priority time to the public worship of God with His family.

211

The third way you must intentionally choose to invest your time is with what I call *Group Time*—time spent consistently in community with a small group from your church. Once again, we see this modeled by Jesus during His life on earth. He spent time alone with the Father daily, and He gathered with God's people for worship weekly, but He also consistently did life with a small group of disciples. In the same way, the early church gathered in the temple courts for worship and then from house to house to do life together in community.

This is important for you, because you'll never develop elements of who you are in Christ apart from small-group community with others. Think about it. Most of the commands in the New Testament can't be obeyed without community. Referring to the list of graces Paul told the church they must clothe themselves with in Colossians 3, Greek scholar William Barclay says it this way: "It is most significant to note that every one of the graces listed has to do with personal relationships. . . . Christianity is community."[3]

The final way you must choose to invest your time is what I call *Go Time*. This is time spent going on mission with God locally and globally. This was the most obvious time modeled by Jesus. His entire ministry was spent on mission with God, and this is also the story of the early church in the book of Acts. The Scriptures record how they spent time joining in God's mission. You can share in God's mission right where you are, but you can't fulfill your responsibility to fully engage in God's mission without intentionally telling the good news of Jesus cross-culturally as well.

As you invest your time in these four practical, strategic ways, I believe you'll deepen your walk with God, grow in community with your brothers and sisters in Christ, and engage in God's global mission in greater ways. It's a great plan to follow.

You may be asking where you should start. Let me suggest a first step I call the 5 Percent Life Challenge. Here's what that means:

- 1 percent of your day invested in God Time. That means fifteen minutes of enjoying fellowship with God through His Word and prayer.
- 1 percent of your week invested in Gather Time. That means about an hour and a half spent in worship, gathered with members of your church.
- 1 percent of your month invested in Group Time. That means about seven hours each month spent in community with people you care about and who care about you, doing life together.
- 2 percent of your year invested in Go Time. That means approximately seven days each year intentionally sharing in God's mission through serving opportunities, trips, and leveraging your job, skills, and passion locally and/or globally.

That's the plan!

Now remember, the 5 Percent Life Challenge is only a starting point. It's not the target. The target is to faithfully follow Jesus by deepening the three relationships we've identified—a relationship with God, a relationship with other believers, and a relationship with the world. But I'm convinced that if you embrace the 5 Percent Life Challenge as a starting point, the other 95 percent of your life will be changed forever as you Abide in Christ, Connect in community, and Share in the mission of God's kingdom.

Best of all, you'll be *unburdened* as you capture the simplicity and purity of living the life of a Jesus follower!

# Notes

## Chapter 1 The Problem: We're Aiming at the Wrong Target

1. Rick Reilly, "Mind Over Medal," *Sports Illustrated*, September 6, 2004, 174.

## Chapter 2 The Solution: It's All about Relationships

1. Mark Lieber, "132-Pound Ovarian Tumor Removed from Connecticut Woman," CNN.com, May 5, 2018, https://www.cnn.com/2018/05/03/health/ovarian-tumor-132-pounds-connecticut/index.html.

2. Spiros Zodhiates, *The Complete Word Study Dictionary: New Testament* (Chattanooga: AMG Publishers, 1993), 936.

## Chapter 3 The Goal of the Christian Life

1. "Currently Held Records," Ashrita Furman, accessed August 5, 2019, https://www.ashrita.com/records/.

2. "Ashrita Furman: Guinness World Records' Most Prolific Record-Breaker," Guinness World Records, accessed August 5, 2019, http://www.guinnessworldrecords.com/records/hall-of-fame/ashrita-furman.

3. Elisabeth Elliot, *Shadow of the Almighty* (Peabody, MA: Hendrickson, 2008), 112.

## Chapter 4 Freedom from "Trying"

1. Jessie Campisi and AJ Willingham, "Behind the Lyrics of 'The Star-Spangled Banner,'" CNN.com, accessed August 5, 2019, https://www.cnn.com/interactive/2018/07/us/national-anthem-annotated/.

2. Clyde Cranford, *Because We Love Him* (Sisters, OR: Multnomah, 2002), 55.

### Chapter 6  You Belong to God's Family

1. John Eldredge, *Epic: The Story God Is Telling* (Nashville: Thomas Nelson, 2004), 20.
2. Robert Waldinger, "What Makes a Good Life? Lessons from the Longest Study on Happiness," filmed November 2015 at TEDxBeaconStreet, Brookline, MA, video, 12:46, http://robertwaldinger.com/.

### Chapter 7  Freedom from Relational Conflict

1. Tom Berman and Alexa Valiente, "When Feuding with Your Neighbor over a Fence Gets Out of Hand," ABC News, January 1, 2015, https://abcnews.go.com/US/feuding-neighbor-fence-hand/story?id=27884426.
2. Zodhiates, *Complete Word Study*, 987.
3. Roy Hession, *The Calvary Road* (Fort Washington, PA: CLC Publications, 2016), 42–43.

### Chapter 8  Freedom from Isolation

1. "Picture of Lonely Grandpa Eating Burger after Grandkids Ditch Dinner Goes Viral," Fox News, March 18, 2016, https://www.foxnews.com/food-drink/picture-of-lonely-grandpa-eating-burger-after-grandkids-ditch-dinner-goes-viral.
2. "Hundreds Show Up for 'Sad Papaw's' Massive Cookout," Fox News, March 28, 2016, https://www.foxnews.com/food-drink/hundreds-show-up-for-sad-papaws-massive-cookout.
3. Aric Jenkins, "Study Finds That Half of Americans—Especially Young People—Feel Lonely," *Fortune*, May 1, 2018, http://fortune.com/2018/05/01/americans-lonely-cigna-study/.
4. Rhitu Chatterjee, "Americans Are a Lonely Lot, and Young People Bear the Heaviest Burden," NPR, May 1, 2018, https://www.npr.org/sections/health-shots/2018/05/01/606588504/americans-are-a-lonely-lot-and-young-people-bear-the-heaviest-burden.
5. Zodhiates, *Complete Word Study*, 873.
6. Hession, *The Calvary Road*, 42–43.
7. Hession, *The Calvary Road*, 49.

### Chapter 9  You Have a Mission

1. Courtney Taylor, "Millions, Billions, and Trillions," ThoughtCo., September 3, 2018, https://www.thoughtco.com/millions-billions-and-trillions-3126163.
2. "Statistics," About Mission, accessed September 25, 2019, https://www.aboutmissions.org/statistics.html.
3. Clifford Grammich, Kirk Hadaway, Richard Houseal, Dale E. Jones, Alexei Krindatch, Richie Stanley, and Richard H. Taylor, *US Religion Census: Religious Congregations and Membership Study, 2010*, Association of Statisticians of American Religious Bodies, accessed October 3, 2019, http://www.thearda.com/Archive/Files/Descriptions/RCMSMT10.asp.

4. Grammich et al., *US Religion Census.*
5. Christopher J. H. Wright, "Whole Gospel, Whole Church, Whole World," *Christianity Today*, September 4, 2009, https://www.christianitytoday.com/ct/2009/october/main.html.
6. Ed Stetzer, "Missio Nexus & Seize the Vuja dé: An Interview with Steve Moore," *Christianity Today*, March 12, 2013, https://www.christianitytoday.com/edstetzer/2013/march/missio-nexus-seize-vuja-d-interview-with-steve-moore.html.

## Chapter 10 Freedom from Complacency

1. "Odds of Dying," National Safety Council Report, February 2019, accessed August 26, 2019, https://www.nsc.org/home-safety/tools-resources/odds-of-dying.
2. Susan Scutti, "Yes, Sitting Too Long Can Kill You, Even If You Exercise," *CNN*, September 12, 2017, https://www.cnn.com/2017/09/11/health/sitting-increases-risk-of-death-study/index.html.
3. A similar quote can be found in Rick Warren, *The Purpose-Driven Church* (Grand Rapids: Zondervan, 1995), 32–33.
4. *Merriam-Webster*, s.v. "light," accessed August 5, 2019, https://www.merriam-webster.com/dictionary/light.
5. Cranford, *Because We Love Him*, 201.
6. Robert Lewis, *The Church of Irresistible Influence: Bridge-Building Stories to Help Reach Your Community* (Grand Rapids: Zondervan, 2001), 48.

## Chapter 11 Freedom from This World

1. "The Future of Teaching the Great Commission: A Q&A," Barna Group, January 15, 2019, https://www.barna.com/research/future-teaching-great-commission/.
2. "Christian Persecution," Open Doors, accessed August 6, 2019, http://www.opendoorsusa.org/christian-persecution/.
3. "Apologeticum (The Apology)," accessed August 6, 2019, http://www.tertullian.org/works/apologeticum.htm.
4. Martin H., Iranian mission fieldworker, firsthand testimony.
5. David Platt, *Radical* (Colorado Springs: Multnomah, 2010), 7, 216–17.
6. Platt, *Radical*, 28.

## Chapter 12 The 5 Percent Life Challenge

1. Cranford, *Because We Love Him*, 107.
2. Justin Martyr, *Ante-Nicene Fathers Volume 1: The Apostolic Fathers with Justin Martyr and Irenaeus*, ed. A. Cleveland Coxe (Grand Rapids: Eerdmans, 2001), 186, http://www.ccel.org/ccel/schaff/anf01.viii.ii.lxvii.html.
3. William Barclay, *The Letters to the Philippians, Colossians, and Thessalonians* (Philadelphia: Westminster Press, 1959), 188.

**Vance Pitman** is the pastor of Hope Church in Las Vegas, Nevada, a church he planted in 2001. He speaks across America and around the world to inspire people to join in God's eternal, redemptive mission of making disciples and multiplying the church among every tribe, tongue, people, and nation. He lives in the Las Vegas area with his family.

# CONNECT WITH VANCE

𝕏 vancepitman

📷 vancepitman

Find out more about

# HOPE CHURCH

VISIT **www.hopechurchonline.com**

**HOPE**CHURCH

Tune into Pastor Vance's
# LEADERSHIP PODCAST

A conversation all about leadership, vision, and
joining in God's activity wherever you are.

———————————

Find episodes at *hopechurchonline.com/podcast*
or on your favorite podcasting app.

# DIVE DEEPER

with these companion resources from Lifeway

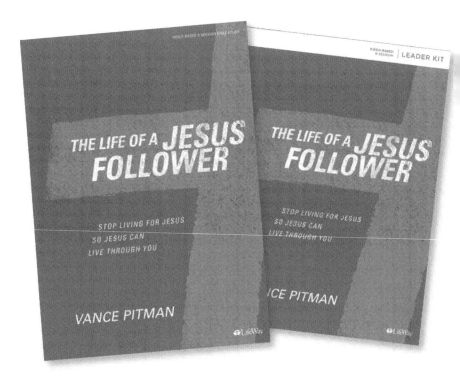

Made in United States
Troutdale, OR
05/06/2024

19685131R00137